Put more
TIME
on your side

SECOND EDITION, REVISED & UPDATED

Put more
TIME
on your side

HOW TO MANAGE YOUR LIFE
IN A DIGITAL WORLD

JAN YAGER

Disclaimer

The purpose of this book is to provide inspiration, opinions, and general information on the topics covered. It is sold with the understanding that the publisher and author are not engaged in rendering psychological or other professional services. This book is not intended to be used as a substitute for therapy or professional support if professional help is needed.

The author and the publisher have neither liability nor responsibility to any person or entity in regard to any loss or damage caused, or alleged to be caused, directly or indirectly by the opinions or information contained in this book.

Typographical or content mistakes may inadvertently be contained in this book. In addition, information may not apply to everyone; it might also be out of date especially because new findings were unavailable until after the date of this book's completion, printing, or distribution.

You may put a great deal of time and effort into reading this book; it still may not give you the results you wish. Neither the publisher nor the author in any way promise time management, productivity, or any other results.

Contents

Author's Note

Thank you for joining me on a journey to better manage your time and your life. I will be your productivity guru. Because you will be investing your time in reading this book, you deserve to know more about the guru you have chosen. Your time management guide is someone who has written five other books on this topic—*Work Less, Do More*; *Creative Time Management for the New Millennium*; *365 Daily Affirmations for Time Management*; and *Creative Time Management, Delivering Time Management to IT Professionals: A Trainer's Manual*—with one or more of those titles translated into many languages including Arabic, Portuguese, Russian, Bulgarian, Vietnamese, simplified and complex Chinese, Japanese, and Indonesian, Spanish, Marathi, and Korean.

I'm sure one of the reasons I have devoted so many of my adult years to mastering time management was the tragic death, at the age of 23, of my older brother, Seth Barkas. I was just 20 when he died from the injuries he sustained from an attempted robbery by a gang. Until that point, like so many young people, I thought life goes on forever. Yes, my grandmother and grandfather had died when I was just 10 and 13, but they were "old." Death, I surmised, only happened to those who had lived a long life.

Alas, when my brother died so young, it was a wakeup call to me that life might not go on forever. My "just world" was immediately shattered.

Each of the time management books I have published reflect my knowledge, as well as what the world was like, at the point each book was researched and released, as well as where I was at that point in my life professionally and personally. Fortunately, by the continued new readership for each of these books, I have achieved my goal of making each book unique, a work that stands on its own. You could read all six of my books, including this one, and get something out of each title, or you could just read one of those books, or even just this one book that you have in your hands now.

For example, when I researched and wrote book number one, *Creative Time Management*, published in 1984, I was a single career woman who had just completed a marathon four years of fulltime graduate school for a doctorate plus working as a freelance writer and college professor. At that point in my life, I did not personally understand the stresses and strains of being a working parent, but I certainly interviewed enough women and men in that situation so I could share in that book about their concerns.

By the time book number two, *Creative Time management for the New Millennium*, was published in 1999, I was a married mother with two school-age sons. The need for "work-life balance" as a working parent had become all too real. But I also interviewed stay-at-home parents for that book so I would not lose sight of those who had chosen a different path than mine, as well as fulltime workers without children so I would be reminded of their time challenges as well. Coaching and speaking on time management provided additional insights into the time management challenges of corporate and entrepreneurial lifestyles.

For book number three, *Work Less, Do More*, published in 2008 with a second edition published in 2012—and a third edition being published in 2017—I was now the mother of two sons who were older and more independent and a grandparent. When book number four, *365 Daily Affirmations for Time Management*, was published in 2011, my husband and I were on the verge of becoming "empty nesters" with only one adult child still living at home, but he was on his way out the door.

When the first edition of this book, book number five, *Put More Time on Your Side*, was published in 2014, my husband and I were empty nesters and my husband had taken a job in a different industry in another city, Nashville, with all the excitement and challenges that relocating causes.

Book number six led me to do scores of interviews with IT professionals for *Delivering Time Management to IT Professionals: A Trainer's Manual*, published by Packt of the UK. Through those interviews and the related research, I got to see time management in a different light. I learned about such specialized concepts to IT like Agile technology as well as the concept of the "death march," all too common in software development. (The death march is what happens when a deadline is so unrealistic but necessary to meet that the IT team has to work around the clock for days or even weeks, often going without enough sleep, eating properly, or getting to see their family.)

For this revised and updated edition of *Put More Time on Your Side*, I did additional interviews as well as the ten-question anonymous survey through SurveyMonkey.com Audience, which I refer to in the book. Rereading my original book and revisiting the concepts and information that I shared, has been a very rewarding opportunity for me, as well as adding vital material to the revised book, especially more on "to-do" lists as well as de-cluttering.

Your productivity guru is also someone who grew up in the U.S.—Bayside, Queens, one of the boroughs of New York City—and has college and advanced degrees—an M.A. and a Ph.D.—and who has been conducting original research on time management since the 1980s, as well as giving seminars and workshops on time management and other topics around the world—including India, Japan, the Netherlands, the United Kingdom, Australia, and New Zealand—and coaching on this subject.

But even more important for you to know is that I feel excited about my role as your productivity guru with this revised and updated edition of this book because I find myself at peace with my own time management skills. I am pleased with the choices I have made in my life as well as with what I have accomplished in my work and in my relationships. I am not filled with regrets like too many I meet who tell me that they are and who, sadly, occasionally will even tear me down for feeling so good about my life. I say to them what I say to you: I am pleased to have this opportunity to share with you in this little book how I have done it so you can hopefully attain the same self-satisfaction that I have worked so hard to realize.

I do, however, have dreams that I need to keep in mind, dreams that are not yet realized. Although I've written several full-length plays, I have yet to see a play produced. Although

I have co-written several screenplays, I have yet to see a film made from one of my screenplays.

These are my own ambitions that I know will be closer to coming true because I am keeping those goals on my radar screen as I work a little bit, now and then, to making both goals happen while continuing with my other professional and personal commitments.

If you want to see an excerpt of my presentation to an association of mutual fund managers in Kolkata in 2010 related to time management and how making time for relationships will even help your business, go to www.youtube.com and put in my name. You will also find an assortment of additional videos of excerpted presentations or TV interviews that I have done.

To learn more about me, you may
also visit my main websites:
http://www.drjanyager.com and
http://www.whenfriendshiphurts.com.
To learn more about my small press, please visit:
http://www.hannacroixcreekbooks.com.

Introduction

Time is the coin of your life. It is the only coin
you have, and only you can determine how
it will be spent. Be careful lest you let other
people spend it for you.
—POET CARL SANDBURG

Over the years, many potential readers of one of my time management books have said to me, with a smile or even a wink, "I'd read a book on time management, but I just don't have the time!"

That was the reason behind this more compact book that you have in your hands, or that you are listening to or reading electronically. I decided to put the key concepts that I know can help someone to become more productive into a more concise book without skimping on ideas. A tall order, yes, but worth it because I know, from my own life as well as from the research I've done or the workshops I've conducted, that time management techniques work!

If you learn, or reinforce, even one nugget of wisdom from this book about how to get more done in less time, you will hopefully consider *Put More Time on Your Side* worth your valuable time.

Yes, it is a daily challenge, even for me, a productivity expert, to make each day meaningful and rewarding. For example, just yesterday I didn't get to start my "real" work for a full two hours after my 5 A.M. awakening. I was at the computer by 5:15, but it was not till after 7 that I *finally* got to the priority task for the day—finishing the rewriting of this book.

What was I doing instead of my priority task? Reading e-mails, sending e-mails, checking on various non-priority work-related tasks, as well as spending just a few minutes, but precious minutes, doing something frivolous—reading posts about celebrities or politicians—as well as something less extraneous—reading articles related to this project.

You know the drill. You've probably done something similar once in a while, or perhaps every day.

But here's the good news: I finally did get down to work by 7 A.M. That's the key. I finally "buckled down" and started on my priority task. There are some who might go till noon, three, or the entire day without getting to that key project that will make the difference between accomplishing something meaningful that day or just treading water. There are others who need to clarify what the priority tasks or projects should be for that day in the first place. Many more know what the priority task is, but procrastination stops them from getting to it.

Once I got to that priority task, I was able to cancel out distractions for many hours and get a lot accomplished. I even had many moments of being "in the zone" or "in focus," whatever term you use to describe that exciting sensation when you are truly concentrating and getting a lot done.

Here's even better news: just by writing down what I did yesterday morning—just by making myself conscious of those two hours I wasted yesterday by examining my actions—this morning I got right to work upon awakening. So now, at 7:45 A.M., I have put in almost three hours of good, solid work time, without the distractions and low-priority time-consuming tasks that I was involved with yesterday.

That is one of the primary goals of *Put More Time on Your Side*—to help you make conscious what you may have been doing with your time in an unconscious or mindless way. By bringing into focus how you are really spending—or wasting—your time, change and improvement is feasible and more likely.

One of the reasons I was able to get to my priority task by 7 is that I was sure what the priority was for the day.

Do you know what you have to do today?

Is it a priority that you set for yourself, or did someone else set it for you?

It is essential that we all take care of the priorities that others require of us. That is how we keep our jobs. But if you *really* want to get ahead, if you really want to have a fulfilling life that enables you to accomplish what you truly want to do, you need to learn how to carve out time every day, at night, or on the weekends for your *own* priorities. It is the priorities you set for yourself, and that you finish, that will make all the difference in helping you to accomplish your short- and long-term goals.

I can think of so many examples of this. Mary Higgins Clark, who wrote magazine articles to support her family, also made the time to write novels, the mysteries that would help her achieve international fame as a premiere mystery writer.

Russian playwright Anton Chekov, who had to earn a living as a doctor, made the time to write the plays that would be his legacy.

Simon & Schuster Editor-in-Chief Michael Korda still made time to write bestselling business self-help books that he intentionally had other companies publish instead of his own house.

I met a photographer yesterday at an art show opening that my husband and I attended in our hometown. She had one photograph in the group exhibit. She told me she is a bartender to support herself but she makes the time for her photography in the hope that someday that will be her full-time job. But she is not just dreaming about doing photography. She's making the time to do it.

I learned early on, when I was raising our two sons, that time management was going to be the way I accomplished things during the hours when our sons were in school. When our youngest was in nursery school, I used those three hours to work on a novel.

As the married mother of two grown sons and one grandson, with a core of devoted friends, a close bond with my older sister, and with a wonderful relationship with my husband, I feel fulfilled in my personal and professional lives. Of course my time concerns are different now that my children are grown and independent, but I still have to juggle the demands of teaching several college courses and being an entrepreneur, a writer, a coach, and a speaker.

The system I call the P.I.E. Technique, which is the subject of Chapter 9, is one of the ways I achieve so much. You may develop your own system. But the key is to figure out not just what you have to do, as well as what you want to do, but, if you're not achieving as much as you know you can accomplish in any given day, learning time management skills that could help you to become more productive. The key is to move along the many projects, or even different jobs, that you are doing so that you work on, and finish, all that is demanded of you or that you choose to do.

Yes, there's always room for improvement for all of us. For the new book on friendship that I am working on, I interviewed a bestselling romance writer, Loree Lough, who has published more than 100 novels. If you consider an author's productivity based on how many books she or he publishes, Loree is obviously more productive than me. So there will always be someone who achieves more, as well as others who achieve less than you. However, that's not the key issue. *We are only in competition with our best self.* Are you doing all that *you* can do? If you could be doing more, or even the same amount but different things, that's all that matters. *Your* reality. *Your* goals. *Your* productivity.

Setting one or more goals for each and every day is one time management skill that will take you far in achieving more in your job and in your life.

There are some of us, myself included, who have been fortunate to be goal oriented from a very early age. My parents were both very goal oriented; my father, William Barkas, was a dentist and my mother, Gladys Barkas, was a kindergarten teacher. For me, goal setting came naturally because of their examples. However, because I am so driven to succeed in my career, I have found that one of the key time management skills I had to learn was how to have a balanced life because both of my parents were workaholics.

That's the power of time management training. You can look at who you are and you can figure out what you are doing based on the habits you developed because of your childhood, school, and even your earliest work experiences. But you now have the opportunity to reassess how you go about your work and your relationships. You can decide what habits are in your best interest to perpetuate and which ones you want to change.

We bring to how we handle our time not just the childhood experiences and the influences of the authority figures and peers who shaped us but also our own personalities.

Anyone who has raised at least one child, or even if you have taken care of an animal from birth, you know that we are all born with a personality that is unique to us. We can, of course, mold our personality if we want to, to some extent, but there are tendencies that we start with and that may always be there. Recognizing what your tendencies are, and working with your inclinations or learning how to work around your propensities, will take you much further than if you are clueless about what is at your core.

For example, throughout my lifetime I have definitely been labeled as a "high energy" person. If you asked most of my classmates from my early school years, probably the majority would have predicted that I would have published at least a couple of books by this point in my life; my writing talents were clear by the time I was ten. But I think it is definitely my time management skills that have enabled me to publish more than 40 books translated into 34 languages and to keep track of those books, as well as the projects that are still "in the works."

Think about your own tendencies. Are you a high, medium, or low energy person? Do you do better working on one thing at a time or juggling several projects simultaneously? Can you concentrate with lots of distractions around you, or do you have to have a controlled and quiet environment?

Leaving a Legacy

In *Put More Time on Your Side*, I am going to ask you to be thinking about your own legacy, whatever your age. Ask, and answer, these pivotal questions:

1. What do I want to accomplish at work?
2. What do I want to achieve in my personal life?
3. What relationships do I value the most that I want to put time into?
4. What is my purpose here on earth?
5. What legacy do I want to leave behind?

Time management teaches us practical skills to get our everyday work and personal concerns accomplished so we have more time to contemplate, and work toward, our answers to those pivotal five questions. It won't answer those questions for us, but at least we will be more likely to have the time each and every day, or at least once each week or on a regular basis, when we are thinking of our answers to those questions and making the time to work on our legacy.

Thanks for reading *Put More Time on Your Side*. You will absorb a lot just by the act of reading. The second step, of course, is applying what you learn to your work and personal time. But the first key step is exposing yourself to new ideas or, if some of the ideas you have read or heard before, reviewing those concepts and deciding which ones you will reinforce. or act on

A Note about Sources

Quotes in this book not attributed to a secondary source are based on original research conducted by this author in the form of either interviews or questionnaires, and are reprinted verbatim or, if necessary, excerpted. If minor editing was required for either sense or clarification, brackets indicate those additions or changes. If anonymity was requested, no name or a fictitious name has been provided; identifying details may also been changed to protect that anonymity. However, care was taken to preserve the integrity of each example. Secondary sources cited within the text have complete bibliographic entries in the Selected Bibliography Including Works Cited section in the back of this book.

I dedicate this book on time management to each and every one of us who still has the opportunity to make our career and personal dreams come true.

Dr. Jan Yager
drjanyager.com

Chapter 1

Why Time Management Still Matters

> Each year it seems that more is expected of all of us in less time and with fewer resources. Competition is stiffer than ever, and getting to market faster and with the right product can make the difference between success and survival or failure.

I had a time management coaching client whom I met with a couple of times. He was one of the top salesman at a risk management assessment company. He was having dramatic challenges with his time at work. I had him share with me how he was spending his day. He was mostly "putting out fires" or doing administrative tasks rather than doing the number one job he should have been doing—getting new clients, generating more sales. To do that, he needed to be making sales calls, setting up, and personally going out on meetings with potential clients.

We discussed all the possible reasons that things had gotten so out of hand for him. He wasn't delegating to others the clerical tasks that others could do and focusing on what only he should do—selling—to bring in the money that would justify his salary and also help him to get ahead at the company. He confided that if his lack of results continued, he was probably going to lose his job.

Upon further probing, I found out that his mother was dying. By sharing with me about that development in his personal life, and his guilt that he wasn't spending more time with her but instead focusing on his job, his wife, and his three children, he was able to see that he might have been punishing himself by unconsciously failing at work.

A few weeks later, I got a call from him. He had acted upon our discussions and was sitting in the parking lot of a company where he was about to go in and make a pitch to a top executive to get that company's business. Landing this company's account would be a huge step in his career. He shared with me that he was nervous about going in and making his pitch. Over the phone, we brainstormed what he was going to do as I reminded him that he had done this before, very effectively, and that he could do it again.

He went in, landed the deal, kept his job, and a few years later he was even appointed CEO of his firm.

That is just one of many examples of how figuring out what you're doing with your time at work—whether or not you're allocating your time in a way that is getting you ahead or hindering your advancement, as well as looking at how you're spending your time in your personal life—can make all the difference in your life.

That's what this book is about. *Put More Time on Your Side* is about taking control of your time so that you can achieve your work and personal goals because you have the power within yourself to do just that! Whether your goal is to become the CEO of your company, start a company, become a bestselling author, get better at juggling a job and raising children, get your college degree or an advanced degree, or switch to some other career or trade, becoming a better time manager will help you to accomplish your aims.

Time management is one of the more popular topics in business today—how to get the most out of each day—as evidenced by the scores of books published annually on the topic and related issues, including such mega-bestsellers as Marie Kondo's *The Life-Changing Magic of Tidying Up*, Timothy Ferriss' *The Four Hour Work Week*, Julie Morgenstern's *Organizing from the Inside Out*, Alan Lakein's *How to Get Control of Your Time and Your Life*, David Allen's *Getting Things Done*, and Stephen R. Covey's *The 7 Habits of Highly Effective People*, to name just a few blockbusters and classics.

So why yet another book on the subject? Because time management does not take place in a vacuum. There are concerns now that were not even on anyone's radar screen a few years ago, or a decade ago, let alone three decades ago when I first started researching and writing about time management. Even though the basic principles of time management may still apply, those concepts need to be reexamined in light of today's world, and new approaches may also be required.

What has changed? Most of all, it's the digital factor, hence the subtitle, *How to Manage Your Life in a Digital World*. Mobile/cell phones and the Internet make it possible to be connected to work 24/7, if you let that happen. In the past, it might be an occasional phone call from work and, if you were in the middle of dinner, you'd tell your family, "I have to take this call," but it was not the 24/7 situation that so many are dealing with today.

When I researched and published my first book on time management, *Creative Time Management*, back in 1984, the world was a much different place. At that time, I was a single graduate student who had just gotten her Ph.D. in sociology the year before. During the four years I was in graduate school, I was one of the first to have a personal computer, an Apple II Plus. That was supposed to make it easier to do the data analysis and numerous rewrites that are necessary to complete a dissertation.

The Internet was not yet a part of my personal computer experience. I was using the computer to analyze my data, but the university library was doing the research searches for me. I would put in a request, tell them what key words I wanted them to search on, and about a week later I would return to get a hard copy printout of the lengthy search. During those years, I was still tracking down the original articles to be read in the physical copy of a journal and other publications that were on the shelves of the library.

I certainly wasn't addicted to the Internet, as I am now, or to doing a search for any and everything on that amazing search engine, Google.com. There are other useful search engines, such as bing.com, msn.com, yahoo.com, to name a few, but I confess that I pretty much depend on Google.com (or JSTOR.com for scholarly searches).

Yes, there are many wonders that the Internet today adds to our life and work, such as split-second research capabilities as well as the opportunity to connect with others around the world through e-mail and instant text messaging and to talk to each other through phone-like services such as Skype or the messaging app, Whatsapp. But back in the 1980s, research was still done the old-fashioned way—by reading books printed on paper that you had to physically go to the library to take out or going to a brick-and-mortar bookstore to browse or buy rather than doing everything from your office or living room through online retailers.

Put More Time on Your Side may be the first book on time management that you're reading, or it may be your third or your eighth. You may already know a lot about time management; reinforcing what you have already learned from other books or from workshops that you have taken—such as the benefits of goal setting and why prioritizing will propel you forward—will still help you to strengthen the positive time management skills you already have. In that way, you will get that much closer to turning around those tendencies that have stopped you from becoming more productive. Or you may be learning the basic principles of time management for the first time. Whatever your knowledge of time management, productivity, and getting more done in less time, hopefully you will find one or many nuggets in this book that make reading it (or listening to it) worth your valuable time.

Are you an organized person? Do you instinctively put things away or, as they say, "everything in its place and a place for everything"? Do you have files all around your office—piled high on your desk, on the floor, or on a chair or sofa? Or do you put away each file after you have used it? Have you gone to mostly filing electronically so you don't even have that many physical files any more, but do you remember to back up your electronic files in multiple ways so if your computer crashes you won't be devastated?

My self-teaching on time management included read-ing the top books in the field when, on November 17, 1980, Prentice-Hall, through my agent at the time, assigned to me that first time management book project. As part of my research, I took my first all-day time management workshop, given by a time management trainer, Peter Turla, who is still delivering workshops.

In addition to conducting in-depth interviews with men and women at all levels of corporations or agencies, from sec-retaries to CEOs, from writers or consultants to doctors and professors, I began my commitment to thinking about time, and how I approached it, so I could become more effective and more efficient so I could teach others those skills as well. For this revised and updated second edition of *Put More Time on Your Side*, I administered a 10 question anonymous survey to 127 men and women through SurveyMonkey.com Audience. (For a more detailed discussion of my background and my various time management books, see Author's Note/My Back-ground at the back of this book.)

The field of time management has continued to soar in popularity since my first book on time management was pub-lished. The relatively tiny discipline of time management has snowballed into a field now known as *organizing* (or "de-clut-tering" as it seems to be called these days) with professional organizers and an international association of its own, the National Association of Professional Organizers (NAPO). It started more than three decades ago, and now it has more than 4,000 members. There's an annual conference and sponsorship of January as "Get Organized Month."

There are even popular reality TV series on "hoarding," which help those who can't part with their clutter. Through an online search, I quickly found at least 20 books on procrastination at a major online book retailer; procrastination is just one of the time-wasting habits that effective time managers need to overcome.

But you don't have to join NAPO, decide to become a professional organizer, or be a hoarder who needs salvation to recognize the value of becoming more organized. The purpose of this book is to help you to do for yourself what a professional organizer could do for you, although you might also consider hiring an organizer to help you set up a system at work or even at home that you then maintain.

"But I Don't Have Enough Time!"

I find it intriguing that when I ask a time management workshop group what is the number one way they could get more done each day, someone invariably responds, "Make it 25 hours long." The irony is that we all know that if the day was 25 hours long, someone would probably ask to extend it to 26 or 27 hours.

For most of us, it's not the number of hours that we have each day that's slowing us down or stopping us from getting more done. We all already have 24 hours and even if we take away 8 hours for sleeping and 6-8 hours for eating, commuting, and interacting with family and friends, that still leaves us with 6 to 10 hours a day for work. How many of us can say that we really make the most of each of those 6 to 10 hours of work time?

If I had to give you two concrete goals for this book it would be this:

To help you to get more done in the 6 to 10 work hours you have each day.

And:

To make sure you are making the right choices so you're doing the right things in the first place.

Doing the Right Things

Instead of feeling like "I don't have enough time," I want you to replace it with this thought, *"I have enough time to get the right things done."*

That is the key to time management and the mantra to this book that I may repeat because that concept will empower you:

"I have enough time to get the right things done."

Setting goals that are based on the priorities in your work is what time management, and being more efficient and effective, is all about.

Some look to the 24 hours that we have each and every day and they smile as they try to make the most of each hour. Others seem to respond mostly to the demands that others place on them; they fail to carve out at least some time each day or evening to get done what they need or want to do. They also fail to keep track of what their own goals and priorities are and to revisit those goals and priorities to make sure that today, this moment, they are getting the right things done. In business, as you know, things can change overnight. It is key to stay up to date about any changes in your field, or at your particular company, that might be impacting on what goals and priorities you need to be setting for yourself.

There are certainly many who are pleased with how they spend their time in one area of their life, such as at work, but not with another, such as in their personal relationships or even making the time to do good in the community. The busy executive who achieves so much for his company but is a stranger to his children. The harried spouse who feels pride in how she handles her job and her marriage, but she feels she doesn't have enough time for herself. The aspiring musician who feels she must put everything and everyone aside if she is to achieve her career goals only to wake up and find herself alone and childless at fifty and wondering how half of her life has flown by. The active entrepreneur and family person who keeps promising to give back to the community through even one hour a week of volunteer work, but he never seems to find the time to do that.

Life management. What a wonderful concept. Taking control of your life as much as you can. Luck and unexpected situations can intervene; you have to deal with the unanticipated when it happens. Whether it's a natural disaster that shuts down the power for three days so your productivity gets thrown off, a sickness in your family, or, on a cheerier note, out-of-town relatives who show up for a visit and you just have to take them in. There are always going to be unforeseen situations that force you to adjust your schedule and even your goals.

Time management guru Alan Lakein says in his 1973 classic book, *How to Get Control of Your Time and Your Life*, that time management equals life management.

But this book takes that a step further. The key theme of *Put More Time on Your Side* is that it is only through *self-management* that you can truly develop time management.

Time management = self-management

Or, to show it more clearly:

self-management
time management
life management

We may all agree that you cannot control everything and everyone. But you *can* get better at controlling yourself.

Think of this as a book version of a life and productivity coaching session. And, as with all coaching sessions, although in this book you will read information, and learn new things that hopefully will be useful to you, it is still up to you to apply what you learn in your own particular circumstances.

There is no such thing as "one idea fits all" the way you might find a sweater labeled "one size fits all." This book offers you an opportunity to consider who you are and to find a way to work within your tendencies or to make changes so that you can become more productive. It also offers you a chance to learn some new ideas that you might find useful in your goal of improving your time management.

The Domino Effect

There's another very practical reason that mastering time management skills will help you in your job or business and in your personal life. That is because time management will help you avoid falling victim to what I call The Domino Effect. Just what is The Domino Effect? This is what happens when you underestimate how long a task will take and you miss a deadline. What happens is that you don't just disappoint yourself, your boss, your co-workers, or even your clients or customers. But the project you had planned to start once that first project was finished is now also put on hold, delayed, or even discarded or scraped because you are late on the first commitment.

Few people have only one or two projects that they are working on, so project three is now moved back or reassigned to someone else. So The Domino Effect is well under way as your credibility is called into question, as well as your productivity and, if you do not get a grip on this situation, even your job.

Of course one solution to avoiding The Domino Effect is to pick a more realistic deadline in the first place. But that will become more likely to do the more self-aware you become as you learn just how long you *really* take to accomplish things.

The other dynamic is to become more effective and efficient so you not only meet the more realistic deadlines that you set, but you even *beat* those deadlines. That will get you a reputation at work of being a go getter as well as someone who delivers "on time and under budget" as they say in Hollywood when they are praising a producer or director for delivering a movie that is not delayed excessively or costing more than projected. But you don't have to work for a movie studio to have your boss find that when you're "on time and under budget" it is a much better situation for you and your career than if you fall into The Domino Effect trap.

Join me as we venture to Chapter 2, "Revisiting Time Management," which offers you an opportunity to briefly review the development of time management and how it has been improving productivity.

Chapter 2

Revisiting Time Management

Time management is even more important today despite all the time-saving electronic devices at our disposal. Being accessible to one's boss or job 24/7 has opened up all sorts of work-life balance challenges. The Internet may make it easier and faster to communicate, but it's also contributed to greater distraction and fragmentation.

When I ask someone what his or her biggest challenge is when it comes to his or her time, this is the resounding answer, whether it's a single woman in her 20s with "only" a job to be concerned about, a busy executive with a spouse and young children at home, or a retiree who has just given up a demanding career as an educator: "I just don't have the time!"

You can see from these examples that the belief that one lacks "enough time" is quite subjective. And that, dear reader, is what we all have to remember about this phenomenon we call *time management*. There is our own perception: I feel I need more time or, by contrast, I feel I have enough time. Then there's the reality: do I or don't I have enough time? And then, there's the solution: I'm going to get more efficient so I accomplish more or I'm going to reframe my expectations and goals so there is more of an appreciation—by me or by my boss—of what I *am* accomplishing.

We sociologists like to say that if you believe something to be true then it's true in its consequences. This is known as the Thomas Theorem, conceptualized in 1928 by W.I. Thomas. The theorem says, "If men define situations as real, they are real in their consequences." So if you *believe* you have enough time to get everything you need to get done accomplished, that will be *your* truth. But if you feel you can't possibly finish all you need to do, that you just can't get everything done, that will dictate your perceptions. This is an oversimplification of the concept that is the theme of the sociological classic, *The Social Construction of Reality*, published in 1967 by Peter L. Berger and Thomas Luckmann. The theme of that treatise is how our socializations, beginning with our primary ones in childhood from our parents, are then impacted by the secondary ones, during our school years, and then, later on as adults, in how we define reality.

Ask yourself how much of your attitude toward time and your basic time management skills go back to your earliest years. Now is your chance to revise those habits and create a new reality for yourself.

In the corporate world, whether you work at the headquarters for a corporation with several thousand employees, you're self-employed and working alone in your home- or apartment-based office, or you work in an outside office with just a few co-workers, there is a lot of initiative required today if you are to land, keep, and excel at your job. Sure, in school you had to study and write reports. But in most schools, including college and even professional or graduate schools, teachers or professors usually provide a written syllabus detailing what is expected of you over the weeks or months of the term.

In the workplace, however, although who you report to might give you some clear guidelines about what is expected of you, there is much more riding on your individual efforts to achieve and succeed. You may be told what your boss wants you to accomplish but *how* you will go about it is often up to you. Indeed, usually the more autonomy you have, the higher up the ladder you will be. With that elevated status usually comes a bigger salary as well as the expectation that you will be a self-starter, a go getter, someone who knows what to do and how to do it.

Unfortunately, you will certainly be told if you're missing the mark and *not* achieving what's expected. Doing what you need to do, as quickly as possible, is usually pivotal for every successful executive or entrepreneur including having superb self-management skills. For those working their way up the ladder, honing more productive ways of going about things will be one of those skills that will get you very far.

Taking time to reflect on yourself is time well spent because knowing yourself is still one of the best ways to achieve more in life and to get more out of your time as you build on your strengths, a concept that will be explored in greater detail in Chapter 4, "Self-management and Self-confidence."

So where do you start on this road to time/life management? Throughout history, philosophers, authors, and just plain simple folk have reflected on time, the meaning of time, and how we should spend our time. Greek philosopher Theophrastus (c. 371 – c. 287 BC) is credited with saying, "Time is the most valuable thing a man can spend." But let's fast forward to the 19th century. The industrial revolution had been transforming the way work was being carried out in England and other parts of Europe and in the United States. Agricultural societies were getting competition from the more frenzied pace of factory life, which was also requiring those who worked in factories to be separated from their families during the workday. Although work on a farm could be a very long day, from dawn to sunset, working at a factory was a special kind of labor. The workday was getting longer and longer, and for some it was including some or all of Saturday and often even Sunday as well.

It became a human rights issue of working a reasonable number of hours because factory work had turned into 10- to 16-hour workdays, 6 days a week. Robert Owen, a Welsh social reformer, is credited with recommending the 10-hour work day in 1810. He also advocated the goal of "Eight hour labor, eight hour recreation, eight hour rest." Women and children in England got the 10-hour workday in 1847 with the French getting a 12-hour workday after the French revolution of 1848.

We find quotes about time appearing in the writings of the American essayists of the late 19th century, such as Henry David Thoreau, who wrote "You cannot kill time without injuring eternity" or Ralph Waldo Emerson, who wrote, "This time like all times is a very good one if we but know what to do with it."

Through the invention of a long-lasting light bulb by Thomas Edison in 1879, it became possible to work around the clock because of the availability of artificial light.

According to Philip Sopher, writing in *The Atlantic*, "Where the Five-Day Workweek Came From," it was in 1908 that an American factory in New England started the five-day workweek. According to Sopher, it was because Jewish workers had to have Saturday off, to observe the Sabbath, and having them work on Sunday instead displeased some of the Christian workers, that the two-day weekend was initiated.

With the industrial revolution, the concept of time management—managing one's time at work for maximum efficiency and accomplishment—became more of a concern among workers and company owners and managers alike. One of the pioneering early treatises to address how to increase productivity was entitled *The Principles of Scientific Management* by engineer Frederick Winslow Taylor. His 1911 book, based on his own observations from when he worked in various factories, professes certain general principles which, at that time, were quite revolutionary, including:

- Taking breaks, rather than working continually, will improve productivity.

- Getting training to further one's skills, rather than just trying to learn on one's own, will enhance productivity.

- Output will be increased by offering "initiative and incentive" to workers.

- Workers should be hired based on their abilities so that they will be more likely to excel if more suited to the work they're doing.

One of the earlier books on time management to reach mega-bestseller status, mentioned in the previous chapter, was Alan Lakein's 1973 *How to Get Control of Your Time and Your Life*. Even though one piece of his advice has never worked for me although it's an admirable concept—handle a piece of paper only once rather than doing the paper shuffle—others swear by that suggestion and I have found his insights into prioritizing enduring.

Psychologist Albert Ellis' *Overcoming Procrastination*, published in 1979, is another classic book to help make the concepts of time management and procrastination lasting issues to be dealt with if you want to become more productive and to have a more satisfying life and successful career.

Over the years, research about productivity has continued to address what habits may help us to become more productive and to accomplish more at work. Outside of this book's concern are the systems about how to make manufacturing more productive such as Six Sigma, introduced by Motorola in 1986 and popularized by GE executive Jack Welch as a way to decrease errors and save money; he used the system to transform GE in 1995. Or the Agile principles that some in the IT field find a useful approach to software development. You should definitely pursue mastering those concepts and that approach, through readings and workshops, if you are in a field that relies on those specialized concepts.

There are other books about time from the social sciences that have made lasting contributions in a more philosophical way, asking us to consider time as a cultural and sociological phenomenon. These more cerebral books on time include such gems as the 1981 sociology classic by Eviatar Zerubavel, *Hidden Rhythms: Schedules and Calendars in Social Life,* or the 1984 timeless work, *The Dance of Life: The Other Dimension of Time* by anthropologist Edward T. Hall.

Some of what you will learn about time management in this book, especially for those who have not been exposed to lots of time management training before, you may find somewhat counter-intuitive. You may, for instance, think that working nonstop will help you to get more done. "If I just put in more hours, I'll get more done."

But the research and real-life examples I have observed usually refute that belief. Not only will continual working around the clock lead to burn out, except for an occasional "crunch" deadline situation, it may increase the likelihood of accidents at work.

Research has shown that taking breaks will increase your productivity, rather than slow you down, and even make you less likely to make mistakes. For example, a 1999 study at Cornell University revealed that if someone working at a computer screen took a break, inspired by an onscreen reminder to take a break, those individuals had 13 percent fewer errors than those who kept working continually.

Time management was the field in response to the Industrial Revolution. Self-management, and getting help to improve your self-management, is a response to the Technological Revolution that started in the 1980s and that we are all dealing with more and more each day as mobile or cell phones, the Internet, e-mail, as well as being able to talk or message internationally have turned it potentially into a 24/7 world. Unless we all practice better self-management, the strides the work world made in getting the 5-day, instead of the 6- or 7-day, workweek, and even the 40 or 30 hour work week, will be eliminated by those who are working 18 hours a day and not even getting overtime for those additional hours. What about those who are failing to

Chapter 3

Time Management Skills That Give You a Competitive Edge

More men are killed by overwork than the importance of the world justifies.

—RUDYARD KIPLING, *The Phantom Rickshaw*

Beyond all the reading you could do through all the numerous classic and contemporary books about time management and productivity, I want to help you jump start your time management skills. Here are twelve key concepts to do just that.

Twelve Time Management Insights That Will Help You to Become More Productive

Looking back on all the original research and coaching I've done on productivity, the observations I've made, and the workshops that I've either given or attended, here are the 12 top time management ideas that, if you grasp each one and put it into practice, you will probably get more done in less time:

1. The number one time management skill is *prioritizing*. Make what you must do the number

one thing you spend the bulk of your time on that day, that week, that month, for as long as it takes to get it done. (What should be your priority? If you don't have a quick and certain answer to that question, this book will help you to determine that.)

2.   It's usually the things you are not even aware of needing to do that sabotage you rather than getting the tasks done that you think you should be doing. So figure out what you should be doing in the first place.

3.   To make optimum use of your time, get to know yourself better. You have to know when you have your peak energy and what conditions will help you to focus. You have to know what technology will aid you and what will shut you down. Put the time into getting to know yourself and into applying what you learn about yourself to how you work and even how you relax and you will become more productive.

4.   Clutter can waste time if you are unaware what is in those piles or if you take longer to figure out what to wear in the morning because you have so many clothes that you haven't worn in ages and that you never will wear again but you still have to go through them to make your choices. So look at your clutter, whether it's books or DVDs, clothes or files, and figure out if it's in the service of what you need to do or it's defeating you

and slowing you down. (For more on clutter, go to the section on clutter in Chapter 5, "Coping with 22 Time Wasters.")

5. Are you doing work that you love and that you feel passionate about, or is it something you fell into to pay the bills? If it's the later, how can you change that? Because if you really love what you do and you're doing it for all the right reasons, you're going to be less likely to frit away your time at work or put off those goals or take much longer to finish that project than you know you really should need.

6. Know where you're starting from. Keep track of how you spend your workdays, workday nights, and weekends. If possible, use a sample. (There are sample logs in the Appendix.) Or you can write in your appointment book or use your smartphone to track your time. You need to look at the wasted time in your day, evening, or weekend. This is for your information alone so be honest with yourself in your recordings.

7. Italian sociologist and economist Vilfredo Pareto (1848–1923) is credited with Pareto's 80/20 rule, which says that you'll get 80 percent of your results from 20 percent of your efforts. The key is to figure out what is the 20 (and what's the 80) and put the lion's share of your energy into that 20 percent.

8. Divide a big task into smaller, more manageable steps. That's the key behind losing weight— I emphasize that in my book, *The Fast Track Guide to Losing Weight and Keeping It Off.* Do the same thing with other challenges, whether it's writing a report for work or a book, giving a speech, or cleaning up your office. Trying to tackle the entire project can be overwhelming and lead to being shut down as well as procrastinating. Creating smaller steps that are more realistic will lead to accomplishing your overall goal in a more systematic way.

9. You can't do it all yourself even if you would like to. The best way to make the most of your time is to figure out what you do best and *delegate* to others, as much as possible, the other tasks that have to get done but that slow you down and are not the best use of your time. And make sure those to whom you delegate know that you value them and appreciate what they do because praise can be as much, or even more, of a motivator than even tangible, materialistic things.

10. Take time each and every day to assess what you are doing, whether you meditate or put a sign on your door, "Do not disturb," and take thirty minutes to an hour to daydream, think, or contemplate. A frenzy of activity may result in getting lots of little tasks done, but you need to concern yourself, each and every day, with the big picture.

11   Remind yourself that *you* are in control of your time. No one else controls you unless you allow them to. Yes, your boss pays you so he or she is entitled to *x* number of hours of your day and days of your week, but you have agreed to work for him or her in exchange for your paycheck so it's in your best interest, as well as your company's, for you to get as much done each and every day as you possibly can. That will ensure that you and your boss and company feel you have achieved more, and that will also help you to enjoy your non-work time more because you will feel that you have earned that break from work.

12.   Finally, and probably most importantly, if you knew that today was your last day on earth, what would you be doing? Where would you be going? Who are the people you would want to call to say goodbye to? Why not take the time today to make a call and say hello to each of those individuals whom you care about because none of us usually know what the future holds.

Delegating

I want to address number 9, *delegating*, in a more detailed way because for so many, especially entrepreneurs and the self-employed, the ability to know what to delegate, and to whom, can make or break your success. Another way that office politics impact on how productive you are at your job is that you need to learn who will help you at work and who will slow you down or even derail you. I shared this anecdote in my book,

Work Less, Do More, but it's so powerful that it's worth repeating it here. Here's what I wrote about that in that book in this section on delegating, "Delegating: Some Final Thoughts":

> Whether or not you should delegate, and to whom you should delegate, can make or break your business. This is a crucial topic and issue to consider. If you think delegating might backfire, trust your gut. I am reminded of a commissioned sales representative that I interviewed who had managed to work for more than twenty years for one entrepreneur. I asked him what were the secrets of his staying power at that particular company. He had two pieces of advice. One has nothing to do with delegating: he positioned his office as far away from the CEO as he could possibly make it so they rarely ran into each other during the work day.
>
> The second suggestion, however, is tied to delegating. For him, it was key to do absolutely everything himself, from going to the post office to mailing out contracts that needed to be signed and returned, to making photocopies. He explained that he did not want his success to depend on anyone else's schedule. If that describes you, and it is not just another excuse for you avoid delegating, even though it might help you at work, and you are doing well, then keep up with your own strategy.

One of my favorite recent anecdotes about how important it is to know what you will delegate, and to whom, is based on an essay I read by the bestselling author Ann Patchett, "The Bookstore Strikes Back," who decided several years ago to co-found a bookstore in her native city of Nashville, Tennessee after the two major bookstores closed down. What makes the success of her independent bookstore a role model for delegating the right way is that Patchett seemed clear about what part she wanted to play in the new bookstore—investor, author, and the store's face to the media. She did not want to do the day-to-day operations of the bookstore. For that, she found the perfect partner in Karen Hayes, who was a sales rep for Random House publishing company when they met for lunch to discuss the possibility of starting a bookstore in Nashville.

The reason this is a role model of delegating to me is that if Patchett had tried "to do it all" as too many entrepreneurs and new business owners feel they must do, it could have adversely impacted on not just the time she had to keep furthering her flourishing writing career but even on the success of the store. Running a store is quite a different matter than funding one or even continuing to write books that would be sold in the store, which of course sells a multiplicity of books.

Of course, not everyone can whip out their checkbook and hand over to someone a check that will cover the rent, inventory, and staffing for a new enterprise. But even if you cannot do that, there are other ways to consider getting help so you do not have to do it all, whether that means trying to find funding through some of the so-called crowdfunding sources that have cropped up, including Kickstarter, Gofundme, or Indiegogo, as well as putting in place a college internship for credit or an apprenticeship program to get help at your company, or even offering a percentage of your company in exchange for services if you enter into a partnership with someone or a group of investors. But check with your accountant or business advisor as well as the employment or labor laws in your town, city, state, or country to make sure of the delegation plans you have in mind.

You can also delegate to technology. Creating, maintaining, and utilizing an up-to-date database is one of the pivotal ways to start and grow your company or business. It can take an individual to input the business cards, or contact information, of those you meet at trade shows or in the course of doing business, but there are also scanning services available that have become much more accurate today. Those services enable you to scan the registration badges of the dozens or even hundreds that you might meet at a trade show and to put that information into an electronic database, such as ACT!, Microsoft Outlook or Excel. You can then use the database with a mail merge function in a service like Constant Conact to send customized e-mail or traditional letters, automating what could have been a laborious task if you had to contact each person individually, one at a time.

The Seven Basic Principles of Time Management

Here are the seven principles of time management to give you the competitive edge in business and in life:

1. Set a goal.

Whether it's finding a mate, getting a degree, finding a job, or writing a report, you need to have a goal—a concrete goal.

2. Create a plan.

How will you achieve that goal?

Create a plan and follow it till you get to your goal. You need to be flexible, however, about how you get there, but unless there is a really good reason for stopping before you achieve that goal, keep your eye on the prize, as they say, and keep going till your goal is achieved. Then go on to your next goal.

3. Prioritize what you have to do.

Making your goal your priority will help you to stay on track when lots of other demands try to pull you from getting your goal done.

4. Pace yourself.

You've heard the expression, "Rome wasn't built in a day." That's a great concept that you need to apply to your time management efforts. Pace yourself so you achieve your goal, as you follow your plan, by prioritizing. If you try to do something too fast, if you rush and don't do your best work, being fast but sloppy or missing the excellence that you could have achieved will disappoint you and those who are depending on you. Efficient and effective requires pacing yourself. Take occasional breaks—during the day, at the end of the day, over the weekend.

5. Be self-directing.

Make yourself the person with the highest standards whom you have to please. Take control of yourself because that will empower you not just wanting to please others.

6. Find mentors, be a mentor.

You need to find others who have been there who can help you to find your way. But don't lean too much on them. They are your guide, your guru, but you need to be working toward becoming a mentor to others.

7. *Reward yourself for each accomplishment.*

The reward system works! Whether it's something really big, such as an all-expenses paid trip to your favorite destination, or going out to dinner, whatever will motivate you is the reward you should focus on. Of course finally finishing what you have to do is its own reward. That's a "given." But something more tangible, even if it's getting a note that praises you from a boss or your client, is still a tangible reward, even if it's not as materialistic.

What's New in Technology

If you use a computer, or a smartphone, you know that the technology advances every couple of months—at least every six months. You may want to trade in your equipment for a faster or better model—getting an upgrade—whether it's for your hardware or your software, or you might want to wait a couple of years until the changes are dramatic enough to justify the cost and the learning curve that something new might mean to you and your company.

In this book, I am not going to try to compete with the online or print magazines or publications that you can access about technology that will help you to be more efficient; the information will become outdated much too quickly. But what I do want to emphasis here is the concept of keeping up, of making sure that you're aware of technological improvements that can help you in every aspect of your work and personal life, whether it's a new online service that allows you to locate a new potential doctor within a certain radius or a website that gives you the opportunity to improve your brain function by practicing memory games.

In the World of Technology, What's New Becomes Standard or Even Old Very Quickly

A couple of years ago, I saw a commercial on television about a small desktop or portable model of a scanner that allowed you to scan in receipts as well as business cards and to transfer that information into your electronic storage system so that you can get rid of the physical papers, or at least store them off-site or far away, eliminating the time consuming habit of sorting through lots of little pieces of paper. Were you aware such a device exists? If you are, have you tried it out yet? If you tried it, did it help your efficiency? If not, is there another system that you might want to find out about that would better for you? Have all-in-one printers that include a scanner made needing an additional desktop device for scanning receipts unnecessary? Are you instead using your smartphone now to take a picture of, and record, your receipts?

Just because what is new quickly becomes standard or even old hat or outdated does not mean you should fail to keep up with new technology that can improve your productivity. With time so finite and precious, anything you can do to get more done without sacrificing quality is worth looking into.

Transportation is another consideration when it comes to time because improvements in what's called "ground" transportation—cars, trains, buses, taxi service, even bicycles—make it worth your time to consider your options rather than always relying on the same old thing out of habit. For example, if you used to fly between Beijing and Guangzhou in China because it took 22 hours by train, as of December 26, 2012, that trip would now take only 8 hours because of the world's longest high-speed train that has started to operate.

With the time required for getting to the airport ahead of a flight, as well as the drive to the airport, which in many communities is located outside of the main part of the city where you might be traveling to, you need to have a time frame that works for you so you can decide if it is more time efficient to fly, drive, or take a train to your destination. Of course, it also depends on other factors such as whether or not there are direct flights or if you would have to make so many changes that it would end up being faster to drive or take a train.

How You Can Try to Stay Current

Reading is one way to stay current about technology and also about what's going on in the world. But asking questions, getting input from others, is another way that too few utilize as much as they could. But of course you have to be careful about what information or advice you receive. I recently visited the website of an apartment complex, and on the website there was a section for resident comments. There are about half a dozen comments ranging in length from one or two sentences to a paragraph. All but one of those comments was glowing and positive. One, however, criticized everything from the building itself, which was found to be poorly constructed so there was too much noise, to a rude staff who failed to address this person's needs in a timely manner.

If that was the one comment you read, you might never go the next step of wanting to see the apartment complex for yourself if you were considering leasing an apartment there. But if you read through the other five comments, not only were all the other comments quite positive, but one reviewer took the time to address each and every negative statement that the other anonymous reviewer had specified.

So the information that others share can help save you time by providing you with their own experiences, but you need to be careful about letting those comments, especially the negative ones, replace your own firsthand experiences that might either refute or confirm what you've just learned.

Here are some tips for staying current that will empower you to be a better judge of the source that you're relying on:

If possible, know where someone is coming from.

If it's a person whose opinion you're relying on, what is his or her background that might predispose this individual to certain preconceived notions that distort the truth? Be observant about the details that an individual provides that might help you to be a better judge of his or her background in voicing a certain opinion. Ask as many questions as you can over the phone, through e-mail or writing, or face to face so you can assess if there's anything about that individual that should cause you to pause about their opinion.

For example, if you're trying to get a consensus as to whether your office would prefer if the office closed down so that they could get the week between Christmas and New Year's Day off to be with their family, you would want to know if your employees celebrate Christmas or if they would prefer to keep working during that time period especially if the days off would be without pay.

Check out if a written source is credible.

When it's a written source—if a comment is published in a newspaper, magazine, or online publication—is the publication known for its accuracy and excellent opinions as well as fact checking of claims, or is it, instead, considered a "rag sheet" that is usually filled with errors and misinformation?

Being in Control of Your Technology

In these days of technology, you definitely have the advantage of using a smartphone to text messages to colleagues or family members and to place and receive business or personal calls 24/7. But you are still the one who needs to make the decision about when, where, and how often you will use this technology to aid, not hinder, your goal of doing a better job at managing your time.

Getting a Better Grip on E-mail

What is the biggest time challenge most of us face today? E-mail. It's a way of communicating that most of us have a real love-hate relationship with. We can all point to times that an e-mail has been the fastest way to communicate with someone. But practically all of us are finding that getting one, two, or even a couple of hundred e-mails a day, including lots of time-wasting spam, can make it frustrating to sort through the forest for the trees.

I'll admit it. I'm addicted to checking my e-mail first thing in the morning. I have a fantasy that a book deal may have been sent from somewhere around the world that I awaken to! But the way I've managed to keep my tendency to check e-mail first thing in the morning from taking over my morning is that I check my e-mails first thing on my iPhone and only open and read something that is a big deal. If I follow up by going online before I get to my "real" work, I limit myself to checking a couple of websites and answering just the key e-mails rather than going through each and every one. Especially if I have a priority task to do (like finishing this book!), I'll allow myself just five minutes to review e-mail. Then, after I've been working x number of hours or getting to x place in my work, I'll "reward" myself for achieving that milestone by taking a break and letting myself check e-mails. I'm in control of my e-mails, however, rather than falling into the "distractionitis" and the "constantly checking" e-mail syndrome, which I have been known to do with very negative consequences to daily output of priority work! (That type of "mindless" e-mail checking usually is associated with a day that ends with me saying, "I was busy all day but what did I accomplish?")

Going back to the mantra behind this book—focus on what you can control rather than expecting everyone else to do things to make you more productive—there are some key aspects of e-mail that you can change that will help you more effectively manage your time and your e-mail.

- When do you check e-mail? If you have priority tasks to accomplish, work on those items before you check your e-mail.

- Time management expert Julie Morgenstern wrote an entire book advocating that you don't check e-mails first thing in the morning entitled, *Never Check E-mail in the Morning*. Would that advice work for you, or do you have to check your e-mail first thing in the morning or your effectiveness would be reduced?

- How often do you check it? If you are in customer relations, you might even be required to constantly monitor your e-mails. But if that is not your job, how often you check your e-mail can be a time saver or a time waster.

- The frequency with which you check it is a key factor in our productivity. Try to check as infrequently throughout the day as possible. Everyone is unique, of course, so determine what works best for you. Over the years, when I give a workshop there's always someone in my class who shares that his or her job, such as those who work the customer service department of a company, requires that every single e-mail is reviewed as it is received. They are judged by how quickly they respond to each e-mail.

- Develop a system that enables you to determine which e-mails you will respond to immediately and which ones can wait.

- The most important line in an e-mail is the subject line. Make it specific and clear. This is your chance to get your recipient's attention and in some cases to even have your e-mail read. If possible, include a time element in your subject line to help move it to the top of the dozens, even hundreds, of e-mails received that day. For example, "Re: 12 noon tomorrow deadline from Chicago Tribune reporter" is much stronger than "Re: Reporter media request."

- Have multiple e-mail addresses. Direct certain individuals or types of accounts or inquiries to one address as opposed to another. (Having a business and a personal e-mail account is another option. Some alumni associations are creating e-mail accounts for their graduates that will redirect e-mails to their graduates' company or personal accounts.)

- Make your spam filters tougher to get through.

- Keep up with your e-mail by cleaning out your inbox on a regular basis.

- Unsubscribe from newsletters, blogs, or groups you have joined if the e-mails are clogging up your inbox.

- Slow down the pace with which you respond to non-priority requests.

- Use your e-mail service's auto-respond function if you're going to be away or unavailable.

- If you prefer to compose a response right away without sending it, put it on a delay, if your e-mail service allows you to do that (AOL® for example, offers such an e-mail delay). Alternatively, save the text of your e-mail to your word processing program, date it, and cut and paste it into an e-mail later in the day or sometime down the road. You can also save your e-mail as a draft in your e-mail program and send it when you're ready to do so.

- Make it a rule that if someone contacts you personally, you will respond or forward the e-mail to someone else to respond on your behalf. If it is an unsolicited e-mail, however, you can determine if it's an e-mail that's been sent out "en masse" through a mail merge program so it is unnecessary to respond to it personally.

- If you need more time to respond, let the writer know that as well: "Thanks for your e-mail. I look forward to getting back to you as soon as time permits."

- Keep it short and to the point but be careful that your "tone" is appropriate and not too "curt" or overly friendly.

- Long, convoluted e-mails may be put aside to be read "later," and, unfortunately, later becomes never. So, if possible, deal with one key issue in an e-mail and made it clear and well-written.

- Your e-mails are a reflection on you just like a memo or a business letter. Make sure you don't have any typos or spelling or grammatical errors in anything that you send.

- For more important and complicated e-mails that are pivotal to your work, compose your e-mail in your word processing program, such as Microsoft Word, and then cut and paste it into an e-mail to send after you've edited or proofread the e-mail.

Getting rid of technology is of course an extreme way of making sure that gadgets do not take over your life. But that is a severe solution, and, if there is a genuine crisis at work or an emergency at home, you will probably regret being unable to get notified at lightning speed.

Instead, try self-management as a way of being in control of technology, rather than letting it control you. You do, after all, have the ability—even if right now you lack the inclination—to turn off your cell phone when you're in a meeting, at the movies, or even at night or on vacation. That's up to you. Does it sound like a challenge you cannot see yourself winning right now? Don't despair! In the next chapter, you will find some insights and tips on improving your self-management.

Chapter 4

Self-management and Self-confidence: Taking Better Control of the Only Person You Can Truly Control

A fool and his time are soon parted.

—ANONYMOUS

At different times in our lives, and even at various times of the day, the time management challenges we face are often caused by outside forces. Co-workers talking right next to your cubicle or outside your office if you're lucky enough to have one, cell phones going off when you're in the middle of a thought, or someone rushing into your office interrupting whatever you're doing with the words, "Listen, you've got to stop whatever you're doing and deal with this order that needs to be completed before the end of the day."

Yes, there are many, many times that others cause us to have time-related challenges. But there are other times that the cause of your time challenges is *you*. *You* cause yourself to shift from one project to another, derailing the momentum you had finally started to build. *You* suddenly feel you're hungry, or thirsty, and you have to take care of these needs even if it slows you down and even if you just had lunch, or a refreshment break, just thirty minutes before. *You* shift from whatever you've been dealing with to checking e-mail even if you know that's not the best use of your time.

This chapter explores ways that *you* can better self-manage yourself, which will lead to more effective time management. It addresses the why before these self-interruptions so you can regain as much self-management and self-control as possible because *you* are the only person who can truly control you.

You will also find help in this chapter so you can see how you can influence others in a positive way so they can become more efficient and productive even if you can't totally control anyone besides yourself. You can, however, play a part in being a positive influence over others, whether it's your co-worker, employee, boss, or even your spouse and children.

Who Am I?

This is a question that is asked in the international hit musical *Les Misérables*, based on the novel by French author Victor Hugo. It is also an essential question that you have to ask yourself if you are to become the self-manager you need to be if you are to be in control of your time.

The more you know yourself, the more effective you can be at handling situations and people because you can work with, not against, your natural tendencies. That is not to say that people can't change; of course, change is possible. But if you at least know who you are in your essence, you have a better chance of making the most of yourself and, if necessary, figuring out how you will change.

Here are some of the key questions to ask yourself:

- Do I like to work alone or with others?
- Do I prefer to do everything myself or to delegate?
- Am I a visual or literary person?
- Am I a "homebody" or do I prefer to be out and about?
- Do I need others to praise me or is it enough to appreciate myself?
- Do I see myself as a "numbers" person or do I think in a more abstract way?
- Do I like pressure or does it stress me out?
- Am I consistent or inconsistent in my preferences?
- Would I prefer to read something on the Internet or view a video about the same thing?
- Do I prefer to read a physical book or an electronic one?
- Do I prefer reading a book or listening to one?
- Do I prefer familiar experiences or trying something new?
- Do I like crowds or to be in places that have fewer people around?
- Do I need supervision or am I a "self-starter"?

- Am I a "team player" or do I prefer to do things on my own?

- Do I need external praise or is it enough to pat myself on my own back?

These are just some of the many questions you can ask yourself to find out more about just who you are and what makes you tick. *The more closely what you tackle in your work matches your personality, in general, the more likely you are to master the challenges and to succeed.* Unless there is long "learning curve" built into a job, the more there is a disconnect between who you are, in your essence, and the demands a job makes on you, the more likely it will take longer for you to master a job as your success is still possible but it will be much harder on you.

That doesn't mean that you always change your circumstances so your deep-seated nature is accommodated so you are more likely to achieve your goals, and faster, but it helps.

Look over your answers to the above questions. Consider the jobs you have had in the past. Which ones worked out the best? What made those situations so optimal? How would you compare those situations to what you see are the traits that you have that make you work best?

Take a few moments now to write down your ideal work environment. It does not matter if this would be a horrible situation to others. If it works for you, that's what counts. For me, for example, although I might like going out of my office to do interviews or workshops, as well as to sit and have a cup of coffee amongst total strangers, I am most productive sitting alone in a room, whether that room is in my house, away from everyone else, or if I have an outside office it is one with a door that I can close rather than in more of a shared office or even a fish bowl type of set up. But if I have to work in a shared open office, I make the most of it.

What works best for *you*? Write down what has been, or would be, your ideal work environment. Include what the office looks like, even your desk, and if you are working for someone or on your own.

The theme of this book is productivity, so I want you to make it a goal to recreate that ideal situation in your current work environment or, if it is so far afield that you have to totally change things, to see how you could alter your situation so you at least start off building on your strengths.

But that does not mean that until you get your ideal work environment you use the fact that your situation is not ideal as an excuse for being less productive than you know you can be. Yes, your situation may not be ideal for you, but you will make the most of it. That is the cornerstone of an effective time manager—someone who finds a way to get as much done (and it is the right things that you are getting done) in the least amount of time.

Work on Your Strengths

The great management guru, Peter F. Drucker, in his classic *Harvard Business Review* article, "Managing Oneself," offers an intriguing point of view that is actually contrary to what so many of us have been told or taught. I for one have always been told that I should work on improving my inadequacies. Learn how to master those skills that are not natural or comfortable to me. According to Drucker, that is a waste of time. It is far more efficient and an approach to work which will have a better outcome if you "First and foremost, concentrate on your strengths" and if you "work on improving your strengths." He continues: "Mathematicians are born, but everyone can learn trigonometry."

Drucker also suggests that you practice feedback analysis to figure out what your strengths are. He recommends that if you have a decision to make or an action to take, write down what you think the outcome will be and then, nine to twelve months later, compare what happened to what you thought was going to happen. Going through this type of an analysis will help you to find out just what your strengths are and put your energy into that. Drucker suggests that one should "waste as little effort as possible improving areas of low competence." He continues: "It takes far more energy and work to improve from incompetence to mediocrity than it takes to improve from first-rate performance to excellence."

The Joy of Routine

Another wonderful tool for better self-management is developing routines that work for you. Routines can be negative or positive; positive routines can provide structure and predictability that, in these days of increased chaos in most workplaces, can be very soothing and helpful to maximize our productivity. The benefits of routine go all the way back to when we were children. Routine gives the child comfort because they feel as if so much in their world is unpredictable. Our need for routine, which does not end even when we enter our teen or adult years, may be one of the reasons that the divorce rate tends to be higher for those who have jobs with schedules that are not routine, such as police officers whose schedules may change from the night shift to the day shift, or doctors who have to answer emergency calls that cannot be scheduled.

Does your job have a routine to it? Your first response might be, "No, I just respond to what's happening each day," or perhaps, instead, you will say, "Yes, I arrive by 8, work till lunch, take half an hour for lunch, and then work till 6 when I leave for the night, putting a couple of hours in on my computer after dinner when the children are doing their homework."

Take a few moments to think about the routine to your job. Routines include everything from when you typically arrive, and what you do after you arrive, to when you have lunch, when you take a break, what time you leave, and even what times of the day, week, month, or year you are more likely to have a work crunch. Figuring out your routine can be very empowering. In my foreign rights work, for example, I have learned that certain times of year I would be foolish to pitch a project in certain countries because everyone working at a publishing company in that country is on holiday. For example, in most European countries, entire companies shut down from right before Christmas until January 7, whereas in the United States, you might find that there is only, officially, a holiday on December 25 and another on January 1, although there might be an extra day off if Christmas Eve or New Year's Eve fall on a Monday. By contrast, in India, where less than 5 percent of the population is Christian and celebrates Christmas, although there is an awareness of Christmas by Christians and other religions, offices do not shut down for one to two weeks as occurs in almost entirely Christian European countries like Italy and Hungary. By knowing those routines, you will be able to plan your business interactions accordingly, leading to a better outcome.

Reducing Stress

How often have you, or someone you work with or care about, told you their hope that it would be possible to eliminate all stress from his or her life? "When I get this done, I can relax," or "As soon as I catch up on all the work I have to do, I'll be fine," or even "If only the clients I have to deal with were more appreciative and polite!"

Of course it is wonderful to reduce stress at your job or in your personal life by becoming more efficient, but you cannot totally eliminate the stress caused by circumstances or others. Instead, you have to improve your coping skills so that the stress no longer gets to you in as debilitating a way as it does now.

Here are some tips from the Eastern and Western disciplines that can help you to de-stress how you approach your work and your life:

- Get enough rest so you are able to take on the world in an optimal physical state. Have you ever noticed how much quicker you react or overreact to pressure if you're exhausted?

- If you drink coffee, tea, or caffeinated drinks, watch your intake so you don't overdo it to the point of getting jittery.

- Practice positive thinking—repeat affirmations or write your own and memorize a few that are especially effective—to keep yourself in a more optimistic mindset.

- Practice yoga or other mind-body activities that have been proven to lower stress levels.

- Count to ten, or walk away and take a deep breath if someone or something is upsetting you.

- Reach out to others for help if the stress is getting unbearable. Call a friend or family member or send a text message to those who will immediately respond to you and who are upbeat, positive, and supportive relationships in your life.

- Consider getting a massage. A trained massage therapist can help you to de-stress. I had a 50-minute shiatsu massage, a Japanese massage technique, at the Stoweflake Mountain Resort and Spa in Vermont during the June 2016 journalists' weekend that I participated in, and it was extremely relaxing.

Empowering Your Mind

There is an increased interest in how to improve memory as one ages; this research is benefiting those of all ages because an enhanced memory is a factor in better time management. If you remember where you put your keys, you will spend less time searching around. If you remember an appointment, you are less likely to either miss it or ruminate over what you should be prioritizing.

Related to memory is concentration—the ability to concentrate and to avoid what is called either "distractionitis" or "fragmentation," the topic explored in further depth in Chapter 8. But here, let's at least mention that you can self-manage your own concentration by the actions you take. From everything that is as simple as clearing the clutter off your desk, including distracting photographs or little knickknacks, as well as taking a priority approach to your day: "I will first get this done and then I'll move on to other concerns."

Concentrating on one task is up to you; if you are assigned multiple tasks and there is no way you can get around having to do it all, you can decide what you will focus on first. Or, if you are forced to juggle multiple projects, you can at least focus on a specific task before going on to the next concern instead of going back and forth, every minute or every half an hour, like the person going back and forth between focusing on a project only to disturb that concentration by constantly checking e-mail.

Self-confidence

The reason self-confidence is included in this chapter on self-management is that by being self-confident you are able to more easily say "no" to someone or something because you are strong in your commitment to your vision for yourself and your time. It also makes you much more focused in your approach to your work and even to your relationships. You know yourself. You know what you need to do. You don't need others patting you on the back or potentially leading you in an unproductive direction because you are trying to get their approval at the sacrifice of your own goals and needs.

Of course this kind of self-confidence is not something that happens overnight. Do be careful, however, that you don't make others feel unimportant just because you are confident about how you want to spend your time. You still want to be polite and tactful. You just don't have to say "yes" to every demand on you because you're unsure about what you know you have to do.

If you're self-confident, if someone asks you to get them a report by 5:00 that day but you know you need till 9:00 the next morning to finish up, you can say that. Instead of saying, "Fine," only to put yourself under extreme pressure to make an unrealistic deadline or running the risk of turning in a report that is not as good as it could have been if you gave it the time it needed.

If you're self-confident, you will take the vacation time that you are allowed rather than fearing that someone will do a better job than you in your absence or that they will decide they don't need you after all. Failing to take vacation time not only negatively impacts on your work-life balance but it can contribute to burnout.

Write It Down

Whether you make notes on your smartphone in the "notes" function or you write things down on a pad or on your computer, you need to keep track of your thoughts. You also need to write down what others say, especially if those words are meaningful or powerful. I started writing things down at a very early age, and I'm so glad I did. Not just because what I might think I thought when I was ten or fifteen or thirty is a lot dissimilar than when I read the words that I took the time to write down at those ages. I can't go back to those ages and stages, even though, of course, as a writer I can imagine what it was like when I was at those points in my life. But writing things down is a way to concretize our thoughts. To anchor us in our own words or the words of others.

Over the years, I have written down the words of others that I want to recall whether it's a family member, like my mother or my children or my husband, or a famous author, politician, orator, or philosopher. And if someone sends me something that is memorable, or meaningful to me, I keep those writings or, if it's an e-mail, I will often print it out and save it.

When I teach college courses, I always encourage my students to take notes during my lectures or when we have a guest speaker. That is because by writing something down it is committed to memory and it is also part of posterity.

When I took a class in art history, I did not just take notes when I was observing a painting. I did little sketches as a reminder of the art work. I got an A in that class and I have those little sketches forever, along with my notes.

When I started spending more time with my mother when she was in her late 80s, I instinctively started writing on my smartphone the nice things she said to me. My mother had been diagnosed with Lewy Body dementia, a progressive incurable neurological disease that would rob her of her motor skills and, eventually, of her memory. In hindsight, I wish I had done a comprehensive interview with my mother about her life, but I didn't think to do that at the time. But I at least started writing down what I called "Momisms" or "Momalies," little things my mother said about me that were positive, as well as anything she said that I wanted to remember because she started speaking so rarely that I wanted to remember for time immemorial. I even dated each one.

So I know that on October 5, 2012, when my mother had one of her moments of clarity, after I said to her, "How'd you get to be such a strong person? I don't know if I could handle what you're going through," my mother replied, "I don't know myself."

I cherish those words because she was so matter of fact and so casual in her response. I hadn't seen that side of her in many, many months.

A year before, when I was visiting, my mom said, "I like to have you here."

Two months later, she said, "You're terrific."

You are so fortunate if those you love don't have dementia! But what that experience with my mother reinforced for me was how important it is for all of us to write down and reread and remember the positive words that are shared with us by those in our educational, business, or personal lives.

To-Do Lists

Related to writing things down is using a to-do list. Whether you write things down on paper or you do it on your smartphone or in a technological system, concretizing what you have to do is a huge time management tool.

In the 10-question survey I distributed to 127 men and women in July 2016, by far the tool that the majority of respondents found most help was the to-do list. A whopping 74 percent found a to-do list the most helpful time management tool. (Followed, way behind, in the number two spot was exercising [30 percent], the number three most helpful tool for managing time was decluttering [24 percent], followed by blocking out time for specific tasks [17 percent], and, rounding up the top five time management tools, going to an in-person workshop [12 percent].)

Tools for Prioritizing: How a To-Do List Can Help*

*This section that follows on to-do lists is reprinted, with permission, from *Work Less, Do More: The 14-Day Productivity Makeover* by Dr. Jan Yager (Sterling, 2008; Hannacroix Creek Books, Inc., 2nd edition, 2012 and 3rd edition, 2017.)

Writing down your goals and priorities helps you to concretize them. The common term for writing down what we need to do is the to-do list. Keeping a list of what you need to accomplish, whether you do it on paper, on your computer, or in your electronic organizer, will help you to prioritize these tasks. It will also help you to monitor your progress. There are all kinds of to-do lists. The basic plain piece of paper with whatever it is that you need to do scribbled on it is a simple version. You can create a to-do list template on your computer or you can buy commercially prepared ones at the office supply store.

To-Do List

Here's a very simple to-do list that includes space to write down up to ten tasks.

Today's Date: _____

Day of the Week: _____

	TO DO	COMMENTS	DATE COMPLETED
1.			
2.			

3.		
4.		
5.		
6.		
7.		
8.		
9.		
10.		

Organizing Your List

Chronological List

You may want to order your to-do list chronologically—that is, according to time, such as from the beginning of the day until late at night. To do so, divide your list to reflect how you arrange your day—before work, during work, and after work. Within each section, follow a simple chronological system. List what you have to do in the sequence you will do it. For example:

During Work

1. Call or go online and make airline reservation for business trip.

2. Write memo for meeting.

3. Get up-to-date distribution list for the memo.

4. E-mail memo to those who will be attending meeting.

Cross off each item as it is completed.

List by Importance

Alternatively, reorder your to-do list by importance:

1. Write memo for meeting today.

2. Get up-to-date distribution list for the memo.

3. E-mail memo to attendees who will be attending meeting.

4. Call airline or go online and make reservation for business trip two months away.

For certain tasks, especially if you are scheduling appointments around your to-do list priorities, estimating how long a task will take is another piece of information that you might want to add to your list.

Crossing or checking off what you've accomplished is another way of reinforcing you're moving along in how you monitor the use of your time.

Some find keeping an actual written to-do list is too rigid for them; they prefer to have a mental to-do list. For others, however, having a written to-do list helps clarify priorities. One executive even noted that without the next day's to-do list by her bedside, falling asleep without tossing and turning throughout the night was impossible.

Typical To-Do List Pitfalls to Avoid

In preparing your to-do list, one pitfall to avoid is failing to estimate how long something will take. Another common mistake is not transferring items you did not complete from your current list to a new list.

To be effective, a to-do list has to work for you. For some, just the act of writing down what they have to do is a reminder, just as a shopping list is a reminder of what's missing in their household that must be bought at the store. By contrast, others need something more elaborate and thoughtful, like a list ordered by priority or ordered by chronology. What's pivotal is that you have a written record of what you need to do and when you plan to do it, as well as when you have accomplished it. This is a way of clarifying your priorities.

Your goal is not to become a list maker but to use your to-do list as a way of more effectively organizing your time. Certain time-consuming tasks will need to be broken down into smaller projects, with each one having mini-deadlines. For example, you may have at the top of your to-do list, "Write report." If that's going to take a week, you should break down that larger task into smaller ones that you can monitor on your to-do list, for example, "E-mail market research company and find out when data will be available for the report" or "Go to corporate library and research latest articles on competing products."

A Powerful Time Management Tool: Goal Setting

If the only concept you get out of this book is that by setting a goal and working toward achieving it you will take better control of yourself and your time, you will have gotten a lot out of this little book. That is because in these days of trying to do too much—a tendency that usually backfires that can be hidden under the term that tries to legitimize this tendency, "multitasking"—setting one goal and achieving it seems, on the surface, to be very unproductive. Why not set three goals and achieve all three at once?

You can achieve more than one goal at a time, but I recommend that you work on one business goal and one personal goal. (And if you are also going to school at the same time you are working, one school goal.) Yes, in the typical school program you will have four or five subjects and you need to achieve your goals for each course, but your overall school goal can be much broader—to keep up with the assignments and get an A.

Similarly, few jobs have only one goal. Your boss probably has five or ten goals for your day, but you need to decide on the one thing you have to get done today, or the one project you need to complete, as you have ancillary goals that may move up in importance on your list once that primary goal is done.

You may also have a huge goal, such as "I want to switch careers from being in the production part of film to becoming an actress in front of the camera." However, within that larger goal there are smaller, interim steps you need to take. Those steps fall under the number two time management concept that will take you very far on your road to improved productivity—break big tasks up into smaller, more manageable tasks. (I remember years ago complaining to my father about how daunting the task of writing a new book seemed to me, and he wisely said, sharing this concept even if the words are not the exact ones that he said, "You write a book one word at a time." The dentist was giving writing advice to the book author, advice

I heeded, advice that has helped me as I have published 40-plus books since he shared those simple yet profound words.)

In my book, *Work Less, Do More*, I created an ACTION! plan that is a wonderful tool to help you in your goal setting. I'm reprinting an edited version of that plan—I devote a whole chapter to it in that book—so you can apply the acronym that follows to your goal setting efforts.

Using the ACTION! System

Most of us in the business world today are in a fast-paced, competitive environment that thrives on results as well as speed. In most circles, just being smart, considerate, and competent is not enough. You also have to generate revenue and keep adding products and customers or clients so your business, or the company you work for, thrives. You and your company need to be financially successful; you and your family are depending on you to produce and to be productive.

How can you achieve and maintain that productivity? The ACTION! system may be just what you need as the catalyst to increasing your productivity. It's a way of looking at what you have to do that is results-oriented, as you get the most done in the least amount of time. The emphasis is on speed and quality. Both are important. Neither should or has to be sacrificed for the other if you follow the ACTION! system for optimum productivity. Let's look at what the ACTION! strategy trains you to do consistently:

A = Assess. Determine what you should be doing in the first place.

C = Control. Take control of what you can influence— your own behavior—and deal with any of the obstacles to working more effectively on a particular task or project that are causing you to slow down or misuse your time.

T = Target. Once you have identified the specific task, project, and/or goal you are going to address today, stay with your target.

I = Innovate. What have you learned about your job, subject matter, or even other projects that you can apply to your own situation, enabling you to accomplish more in less time? Don't be afraid to try new systems or ideas (or go back to the tried and true ones that worked for you in the past).

O = Organize. Use organizing strategies that allow you to accomplish your goal better and faster. Group similar tasks together. Organize your files, books, and supplies. Spend the time to keep your database up to date, as this will save you time when you need to find a person, place, or information that is pivotal to the task at hand.

N = Now! The key to the ACTION! strategy to help you to become more productive and effective is to address your key priority concern *now*, not tomorrow or after you've done a million other less important things. The N for *now* is a reminder that you need to stop procrastinating, making excuses, distracting yourself, and putting everything and everyone before taking—and completing—the ACTION! that will move this project, and your career, along.

For a sample ACTION! worksheet that you can use for your own goal setting, go to the Appendix.

SMART Goals

Let's also look at the very popular SMART acronym that many time management experts and coaches uses in their goal-setting work. I didn't create that acronym, the way I created the ACTION! plan one—SMART is generally attributed to George T. Doran going back to 1981 in Spokane, Washington, But I want to share SMART with you because it's another valuable tool in your goal setting.

S = Specific

Yes, you need to make your goal concrete and not so amorphous that it's hard to get a handle on it. A publicist might set as her or his goal, "Contact 25 members of the media via e-mail and phone today" versus "Contact the media."

M = Measureable

As you see from the above example, by quantifying the goal—contact 25 members of the media—it's much easier to see if, by the end of the day, you've achieved your goal. If you're an insurance salesperson, your measureable goal might be, "Call 10 potential new clients by 5 p.m. today."

A = Achievable

Consider your day if this is a daily goal. Divide up your day into hours and consider how long your typical call or e-mail takes for you to do. Can you achieve the goal you are setting for yourself?

R = Realistic

This is very much related to the previous concept of *achievable*. Think about your past performance. If, even when you were working at your maximum efficiency, you could only call five possible new insurance clients in one day, setting a goal of ten just might be so unrealistic that instead of being a possible goal that inspires you, it will "shut you down."

T = Time Framed

Open-ended goals are less effective than those with a time frame. "I will lose three pounds by the end of this month" is a time framed goal. "I will lose weight" is open-ended. "Finish report" is an open-ended goal without a time frame. You are much more likely to achieve that goal if it is stated in this way: "Finish report by 2 p.m., reread it, check it for typos or spelling errors, make any corrections, and turn in at 4 p.m."

Voila! You achieve your goal. What next? You work on your new goal.

The beauty of goal setting and developing an ACTION! plan that helps you to achieve each and every goal is that you are taking control of your time and your life. You are not feeling out of control, only reacting to each and every e-mail that is sent your way. Nor are you letting yourself wander away from your own priorities as you find yourself falling into the "busy but unproductive rut" that can sabotage your career and personal goals and accomplishments.

So now you have your ACTION! plan and you've applied the SMART goal-setting strategy to it, fine tuning it so you have a maximum chance of achieving your goal. But you're still not as productive as you'd like to be. Consider if one or more of the 22 time wasters discussed in the next chapter are slowing you down. You'll find possible solutions to overcome each one.

Chapter 5

Coping with 22 Time Wasters

Any habit that stops you from getting to do what you truly want to do is a time waster. Fortunately, you can overcome each and every one. The first step is to recognize what your particular time wasters are. The second step is to understand the underlying causes. The third, and pivotal, step is to eliminate each and every one.

It is my observation that most time wasters fall into five categories—mental, emotional, physical, structural, or logistical. If you can conquer your own thoughts and feelings, you can conquer and control how you spend your time.

In the mental arena are these typical time wasters:

- Letting your mind drift (poor attention or poor concentration)
- Making excuses

In the emotional area are these concerns that can slow you down if unchecked:

- Jealousy
- Insecurity
- Procrastination
- Perfectionism
- Fear of completion
- Fear of failure
- Fear of success

Keep in mind how physical conditions can impact on your time, including:

- Inactivity
- Obesity
- Exhaustion (not enough sleep)
- Pain
- Lack of energy

The structural and logistical time wasters are probably the easiest to overcome. Here are the key structural ones:

- Equipment breakdowns
- Backup failures

Finally, the logistical ones require a change in how you go about your work if you are to conquer these time wasters, including:

- Over-scheduling
- Unrealistic deadlines
- Poor planning

- Inadequate pacing
- Lateness
- Clutter

Let's look at what causes each of these situations and how to overcome each one so you can gain better control of your time life.

Mental

Letting Your Mind Drift (Poor Attention or Poor Concentration)

We're going to assume that you do not have ADHD (Attention Deficit Hyperactivity Disorder). We're going to assume that you simply are in that vast category of workers or students for whom staying focused has become a huge challenge.

What is the cause of this tendency? Doing too many things at once. Unfortunately, in an effort to please your boss and everyone else who is making demands on you, you are failing to focus on your one priority task.

What can you do to overcome this "letting your mind drift" tendency? First of all, pick one priority task and work on that as much as you possibly can. Second of all, make your work environment as distraction-free as possible. Remove all the family photographs that populate your desk or are pinned to your wall if you have a cubicle. Third of all, if necessary, work when others are busy or absent so they can't distract you, whether that means you go to lunch at 1 so you have the hour from 12 to 1 when everyone else is at lunch to be focused, or you arrive earlier or stay later. (But only, of course, you have permission from your supervisor or boss.)

Fourth, and even better than that last suggestion or solution, is for you to remind yourself that you are in control and you are capable of concentrating. Even surrounded by others, focus.

Finally, what are the rewards if you finish this project and don't let your mind drift? Reinforce that for yourself to motivate yourself to stay on track.

Making Excuses

Aren't you sick of the excuses of others or telling others why you can't do something? Whether the reason someone's late with something is blamed on the weather or on someone else, it's still an excuse. Of course things happen that can cause you to miss a deadline or forget an appointment, but in the interest of the most pivotal theme of this book, that time management is really life management, it is key that you take responsibility for your behavior and stop making up, or sharing, excuses to explain away why you did not do something you were supposed to do or perform at your optimum level. Instead of wasting all that time with excuses, put your energy into accomplishing what you have to do as quickly as possible. That's what people really want to hear, not your excuses.

Emotional Time Wasters

Jealousy

It's okay to be jealous, just don't let it eat you up inside. If you stop feeling bad about your jealous feelings, you will free up a lot of time—time that you can spend working harder to get for yourself what it is that someone else has that you are so jealous about.

I don't know about you, but I find it refreshing when someone admits to his or her jealousy. Once again, I'm talking about just talking about the jealous feelings, not doing something stupid or contemptible like acting on those feelings in a fit of rage. That's dysfunctional and not at all in anyone's best interests.

But admitting to your jealous feelings can be very freeing.

Have you ever been blinded by jealousy? Has anyone ever been consumed with jealousy for you? If you've experienced that kind of jealousy or been the recipient of it, you know how debilitating jealousy can be and how it can eat up your time and energy.

Accepting that jealousy is normal and recognizing that you're feeling it, or someone is feeling it toward you, without diminishing what you are doing, what you need to do, or what the other person has achieved will take you further than if you try to deny the feelings or pretend that jealousy either doesn't happen or is something that's bad and to be avoided at all costs.

Insecurity

Feeling secure within yourself stems from two sources— what you learned about yourself during your formative years and what you know, realistically, is true now. If your parents and other authority figures made you feel like you had value and skills, and praised you appropriately, you will probably have a deep-seated sense of security. If, by contrast, you were constantly put down and berated, you may feel insecurity, even though you know the feeling is not based on what you have achieved.

How do you overcome this type of deep-seated insecurity that rarely has to do with what was true about you when you were growing up? It's usually more of a reflection of the security or insecurity of your parents or others around you who found that putting you down, sadly, made them feel more powerful because they were actually insecure about their own capabilities.

The way to get over this type of deep-seated insecurity from childhood is to consider going into therapy and looking at the causes and realizing that you have earned feeling good about yourself. You can also try to overcome it on your own by using self-talk: "I am talented. I am attractive. I am smart." Or you can read books to help you overcome this type of insecurity, self-help books that will walk you through tossing aside the outdated and unfair putdowns from family or even from schoolmates or bullies, so you can be much more effective and self-affirming today.

You can become secure and self-loving, rather than self-loathing, today. If you're currently alone and lonely, finding and cultivating friends or romantic partners who treat you with love, affection, and respect can also help you to feel more secure about yourself. The thinking goes: If those you like also like you, there must be something likeable about you! If you hang in there with those who treat you well and make you feel good about yourself long enough, you may start to believe them yourself!

The other kind of insecurity is a healthy way of telling you that you don't know as much as you need to know to get a job done. That is actually a good, productive insecure feeling. What is the cure for that type of insecurity? Doing the work, hiring the expert, or mastering the skill so you earn feeling secure.

Anxiety

Practically everyone has the garden variety of anxiety, or being in a state of worry, from time to time. Whether it's because of a new boss who's placing excessive demands on you or a co-worker that you fear wants to get you fired so he can get your job, anxiety is just part of all of our lives. When it takes over, however, and is so extreme as to become debilitating, then it is a time waster that needs to be understood and addressed.

If your anxiety is so overwhelming that it's hard for you to get out of bed in the morning or to get to work, you might want to consider finding a trained therapist—psychiatrist, psychologist, or social worker—to work with you to understand the reasons behind your anxiety as you overcome it.

If your anxiety is something you think you are able to control on your own, use positive self-talk to help yourself to move forward with your obligations rather than getting shut down and slowed down unnecessarily or excessively.

Depression

Depression is a powerful feeling that all of us have had from time to time. If it's occasional or mild, especially if it's tied to something that's happened whereby depression is a predictable and normal response, such as breaking up with a boyfriend or girlfriend or the death of a family member or a pet, and if it seems to dissipate on its own after a reasonable period of time, anywhere from a couple of days or weeks to a month or more, it may not be a chronic state. But if it is chronic and ongoing, you might want to see a therapist for help as well as consider getting anti-depression medication if you are a candidate for that type of treatment. (There are potential serious side effects to all anti-depression medications, including personality changes that can occur when you first start taking the medication, while you are taking it, and after stopping it, so you need to be under a doctor or therapist's care. You should not be self-medicating.)

Time may seem to stand still when you are depressed. If you have lost a loved one, it may seem as if all the activities you used to do, including working, temporarily lose meaning for you. You may feel as if it takes all your energy just to get through the day. Your feelings are so powerful that at least for a certain period of time you need to focus on feeling less depressed rather than being more efficient.

That's just fine because depression, especially if it's prolonged, is a very serious emotional state that needs to be addressed and treated. Dealing with your depression, if you feel depressed, is your number one priority; becoming more efficient can wait till you're feeling better emotionally.

Procrastination

I always tell myself and others that procrastination can also be seen as information. What are you putting off, and why? If you can get at the bottom of that by asking and answering those two questions, you have a better chance at coping with your procrastination and overcoming it than if you just feel bad about yourself because you're delaying what you know you have to do.

What are you procrastinating about? Of course, the no-brainer answer is that it's something you don't want to do, but that's too easy an answer. Why don't you want to do it? Is it too hard? Too boring? Is it something that someone else, besides you, should be doing in the first place?

Why are you (or someone else) procrastinating? Is there something about the project that is wrong or some information that you lack that you need to first obtain so you can finish up a job?

What are the *benefits* to you of procrastination? Does it get you attention, albeit of the negative kind, but perhaps it's attention that you lack and crave more than handing something in on time and getting praise?

Procrastination, especially if it's controlled procrastination that's conscious rather than uncontrolled unconscious procrastination, may actually be a useful thing, not a time waster. Rushing into things without everything that you need can have even more negative consequences than procrastinating. You have to decide if your procrastination is justified and positive or negative and something to be avoided or dealt with.

Over the years, I've suggested as one of the ways of dealing with procrastination what I call *creative procrastination*. The difference between creative procrastination and plain old-fashioned procrastination is that you substitute another priority task for the one you should be doing that you're putting off. You are getting your priorities done, just in a different order. (You're not procrastinating by doing something unproductive or even self-destructive like overeating or over-spending to avoid doing what you have to do.)

I found out, however, to some, the concept of creative procrastination can be very intimidating and stressful. Those individuals are from a very rigid, "do one task until you finish it" school of time management. That's just fine for them, and if you're in that group for whom that philosophy is absolutely pivotal, by all means stick with it. Creative procrastination can, of course, be something that could get out of hand, and before you know it you could get into a "doing too many things at once" type of time-wasting situation.

But if you use creative procrastination only occasionally and you keep control over it, it can lead to finishing several goals, albeit in a different order, rather than just being blocked and unproductive for short or longer periods of time.

There's also a modified type of creative procrastination whereby you don't switch to a completely dissimilar project; you do something else related to that same project, just picking something that you are not blocked on. For example, if you have to write a report and you're blocked on the opening, you work on the conclusion or the bibliography.

Some other solutions if you're plagued by procrastination?

- Try using a timer. Set the timer and tell yourself, "I'll just work on this for thirty minutes." You may be amazed that when the timer goes off, you're "on a roll" so you decide to keep going. Don't have a timer handy? If you have a smartphone, like an iPhone, you will find a timer as part of your clock function. You can also use an old-fashioned wind up kitchen timer if you happen to have one available.

- Try the reward system. "If I do *x*, I'll reward myself with *y*." Make the reward something that will motivate you. Promising yourself that you'll do filing if you make one more phone call to try to get new clients will probably not be a great reward.

- Give yourself permission to put something off. Procrastination might be a way of your mind, or your body, telling you that you need a break.

- Allow yourself to take a break but give it a
  finite time.

If you're finding your delay is getting out of hand, give it a specific time frame. "I'll take an hour off to exercise and then I'll get back to work" or "I'll walk around for ten minutes to clear my head and then I'll go back to preparing for that meeting."

Perfectionism

Were you raised by a perfectionist? If you were, you know that if you got 98 or A- on a test, that parent wanted to know why it wasn't a 100 or an A+. If you have a perfectionist for a boss, if you turn in something that is terrific, he or she will always find something wrong about it, either requiring a do-over or just giving negative feedback because whatever you did was not perfect.

Perfectionists, or those who were raised by perfectionists, learned that, unfortunately, they were not deserving of unconditional love. They had to earn their parents' love based on their performance, and if the performance was not perfect the love was withheld.

The frustration is that perfection is, unfortunately, in most cases unrealistic. I always say that you should aim for excellence, not perfection. But then I quickly add, in my attempt at humor, that you will want your surgeon to be a perfectionist, as well as your proofreader.

Those are two extremes, however. Most jobs will do just fine with the standard of excellence.

So how does being a perfectionist or working for a perfectionist slow you down and interfere with more effective time management? Perfectionists are usually a pretty unhappy lot because the approval they feel is fleeting, lasting only as long as the praise and the perfection they have achieved in that instant, which does not last very long.

To deal with perfectionism is to look at the trait head on and to be aware that you are like that and that it is in your best interests to change. That's something else, of course, than if you work for a perfectionist and you have to work around that situation because you can't change the perfectionist (unless he or she wants to change). So if you work for a perfectionist, you have to learn not to take their criticism and their emphasis on perfection personally. It's their perception of things, but you do have to try to be as perfect as you can so you don't unwittingly intensify things by confronting the perfectionist about his or her unattainable and unrealistic standards.

Fear of Completion

Fear of completion is tied to one of the emotional time wasters that I previously discussed—insecurity. If you are insecure about the results of your efforts, you will consciously or unconscious delay finishing so you do not have to be judged. Fear of completion is also tied to perfectionism. If you think your effort has to be perfect, you will delay completing a project; if you don't complete it, it can't be imperfect.

As you did with procrastination, figure out what benefits you are getting from failing to complete something. Emotional benefits. You are probably suffering a lot in terms of wasted time and career paralysis. But ask yourself what you are avoiding facing by failing to complete a specific job. Figure out the answer to that and decide if you can deal with facing the consequences of completion on your own, or if you need to work with a therapist or a coach, so you will overcome this time waster.

Fear of Failure

I've written about fear of failure before, but this time waster and its companion time waster fear of success are too pivotal to avoid including in this book. How does fear of failure waste your time? If you're afraid of failing, you're going to delay things because if you keep putting something off—so the person with this syndrome thinks, on an unconscious basis, of course—you can't be "bad" because you haven't yet been judged.

Unfortunately, by delaying and missing deadlines and not having projects or work that can be submitted in a timely fashion, you unwittingly bring about the very situation you fear. The delays either make you fail or increase the likelihood that you, or your work, will be seen in a negative light.

Someone who fears failure is insecure and afraid of being judged. To get over this time waster, work on your self-esteem and self-confidence. Feel that you and your work are excellent and you will be less likely to fear failure and to delay submitting your work.

If you're still insecure, at least budget extra time to show your work to those whose opinion you value. Getting praise or even helpful feedback from others before you have to submit your project or work may help you to get over your fear of failure.

Fear of Success

Unlike the person who fears failure, the person fearing success actually thinks that he or she will show up someone else whom he or she feels will then withhold their love because they have been put in a less favorable light. Once again, this is an unconscious fear that motivates the person with this time waster to put off finishing projects or even doing a less than optimal job.

In this case, in order to overcome this fear, you need to work on improving the relationship you have with the person whom you fear will abandon you if you show him or her up. If you feel more secure about how they feel about you, you won't be worried that being better at your skills, whatever that might be, will lead that person to abandon you.

You do, however, have to also do self-talk, or seek out the help of a professional, if you need assistance learning how to cope with the possibility that your beloved will pull away or abandon you if you are more successful than him or her. That may not happen, but if your worst fear is realized you need reassurance that you will be able to handle it.

Diminishing yourself or your talent and putting off finishing tasks, or showing the world what you are good at, because you are afraid of the success will slow you down until you deal with this challenge.

Fear of Delegating

The reason a fear of delegating is a huge time waster is that if you try to do everything yourself, you will be avoiding the key productivity principle of focusing on your strengths. You will find yourself doing everything from making every single phone call to scheduling your appointments. Now you know from the previous discussion in Chapter 1 that there are those for whom doing everything yourself is a key to their success. Those individuals, however, are few and far between. For most of us, if we try to do everything, we will get sidelined by the details as we start missing the big picture.

Being able to delegate is one of the cornerstones of the advice behind Timothy Ferriss' mega-hit book, *The Four-Hour Work Week*. With the money he made selling vitamins over the Internet, he learned to delegate to others those tasks that he did not have to do, freeing himself up for what he was best at as well as what he really enjoyed doing, like writing books and speaking.

Harvard Business School professor, author, and business consultant Robert Pozen in his book, *Extreme Productivity,* shares his three big ideas for productivity. The third idea is actually tied to delegating as that concept is to "don't sweat the small stuff." He continues: "Deal with low-priority items in a way that allows you to spend as little time on them as possible." (His other two big ideas are to "articulate your goals and rank in order of priority" and "focus on the final product.")

One way for low-priority concerns to take *less* of your time is if you're delegating those concerns to others (to individuals or to technology).

But why would someone be afraid to delegate? I'm sure you've heard the expression that someone's a "control freak." Those who are afraid to delegate may need to do everything themselves because they distrust the skill level of others.

It might also stem from insecurity; the person who fears delegating might be afraid that the person to whom they delegate will show them up and they will be replaced. Of course, this sometimes happens as we have seen replacements for major morning TV show hosts who go on vacation or on assignment and find themselves permanently replaced by their alternates because the viewer response to their replacement was so much more positive. But those examples are rare. Most of the time, you are delegating a task to someone because you have diverse skills and it is a waste of your time to be doing a task that someone else could do better. Often it is a skill that requires a very different type of skill set than yours, so you need not fear being replaced by the person to whom you are delegating. For example, if you are excellent at writing copy for advertising, you will be focusing on doing that task and you will delegate to someone else database management, which is a necessary task but one that requires a special type of skill.

The distrust that is behind a fear of delegating is that you do not think the person you delegate to will do a good or excellent job. In order to overcome that fear, you need to gain confidence in your ability to select the right person to whom you delegate in the first place. You also need to have checks in place so that, especially in the beginning, you are making sure the person to whom you are delegating is getting it right. It is not distrustful to be checking up on the person to whom you are delegating. That is your job because, as they say, the buck always stops with the supervisor. The frequency with which you check the work of the person to whom you delegate may change, but you will still want to keep checking. If you delegate effectively, however, the checking over and verifying that your delegation system is optimal will *not* take as long as if you did the work all yourself.

For example, let's say it takes you fifteen minutes to read over the report of the person to whom you delegated writing the report. You know, from past experience, that it would have taken you one to two weeks, working five to seven hours a day, to research and write that report to begin with.

Physical Time Wasters

Inactivity

Walking or running is easier if you're in shape. If you have to catch a bus or walk to your car, you will get there faster if you are exercising regularly, improving your physical stamina.

You don't have to join a gym to get active. You can just walk more, or you can even work out to music in your apartment or house. You can join a sports team as a way of getting more active; a 27-year-old I know is part of a weekly dodgeball league that certainly offers him a regular active workout.

Obesity

Being overweight or obese will definitely slow you down, and if you fail to get a grip on this physical challenge it can cut years or decades off your life expectancy. According to the Harvard School of Health in an online report entitled "The Obesity Prevention Source," the health consequences of obesity are extreme and numerous ranging from an increased risk of cancer, heart disease, and diabetes to infertility and even depression.

Exhaustion (Not Enough Sleep)

We have learned that pulling the "all nighter" to get a lot more done by failing to sleep is not just a time waster but a potential health hazard because you could fall asleep at the wheel when you're driving without sleep, or you are more likely to have accidents if you are exhausted and not properly rested.

Figure out how much sleep you need by letting yourself sleep till you're no longer tired rather than waking up only to an alarm clock. Once you see what your ideal pattern is, then set the alarm clock and go to sleep and wake up according to that optimum pattern.

Pain

Pain will slow you down whether it's a toothache or a shoe that's too tight so that your toes are pinched and in pain.

Figure out what is causing the pain and deal with it so you are more efficient and effective.

Lack of Energy

In their article in the *Harvard Business Review*, "Manage Your Energy, Not Your Time," Tony Schwartz and Catherine McCarthy of The Energy Project share what they discovered based on five years of working with thousands of managers and leaders—working longer hours does not work because energy is finite but energy can be renewed. To accomplish that, they recommend revitalizing personal energy by working on these four types of energy:

1. Physical

2. Emotional

3. Mental

4. Spiritual

Structural Time Wasters

Equipment Breakdowns

If you can afford it, have backup equipment because breakdowns are inevitable and that can really slow you down. Have a second computer in case your main computer needs to be repaired. Have a backup printer as well.

If you drive a car to work, it may be unrealistic to have a second car if your primary car breaks down, but at least have the phone number handy of a taxi service or even a couple of friends or neighbors who would be willing to pick you up and get you to a meeting or your office.

Backup Failures

I back up what I am writing on my computer as often as possible, especially with essential time-sensitive and major projects, in at least three ways, sometimes four:

1. On my main computer, on the hard drive.

2. On either a flash or thumb drive or an external hard drive.

3. I back up to the "cloud" that the computer provides as part of the system.

4. I send the files to myself through the Internet periodically so if the hard drive crashes and the backup alternative drive gets lost or crashes as well, there's at least some version of what I'm working on in cyberspace so I don't have to start from scratch.

5. A hard copy that's printed out. (In the interest of trees and to avoid the cost of having to buy all that paper or to file the various drafts of a project, I'm trying to get away from printing out unless it's absolutely necessary. Still, it is a nice additional way to back up that is tangible.)

6. You can subscribe to a cloud or backup service that provides you with online storage of some or all of your files.

7. Dropbox is one of the Internet services that enables you to store key files permanently that you can have access to from anywhere, even if your personal computer crashes.

How and when do you back up? I hope you do it regularly. Do you periodically go through your backed up files to see what you have and to sort, sift, and purge so you're in control of your backup system?

Logistical Time Wasters

Over-scheduling

Here's an anecdote from the London Book Fair that I think you will relate to: I was so impressed with how efficiently I thought I had put all the key appointments into portable schedule so I didn't have to carry my heavy appointment book around with me on the second day of the fair. I consulted my schedule and moved from meeting to meeting, proud of how I didn't "overbook" and even allowed myself a nice break for lunch!

Alas, almost at the end of the day, I see the booth number for a company and what suddenly flashes through my mind is that I was supposed to meet the father of the exhibitor at that stand—my first publisher in the UK—for a quick lunch, and I had completely forgotten about that appointment. It turned out I had not copied over all the appointments from my master appointment book into my portable schedule! The schedules did not match!

I of course apologized in an e-mail later that evening very profusely about that missed appointment and the three others I had completely missed, and everyone was polite and understanding, but I wondered, "If I did this, and I'm a productivity expert, what are others doing?"

It was a very humbling experience because, over the years, others have been "no shows" at meetings and I never heard from that person again. I could see that it's possible they were so embarrassed, as I was, that they preferred to just ignore the whole situation than admit that they had made a mistake.

But I also felt humbled by the experience because I saw that in today's busy, hectic world, making mistakes like that is probably happening more often, rather than less frequently, because we're tempted to over-schedule in our haste to pack more opportunities into our business trips.

To avoid over-scheduling, be more realistic about just how many appointments you can handle, including giving yourself adequate breaks between appointments as well as "down time" so you can also have the serendipity that can occur in one's day whether you are just at the office or at a conference. If every single minute is scheduled, it is more likely that it will all blend together and become a blur. Also, you will not have time to re-energize yourself, which can make the difference between performing at your optimum or being exhausted and overwhelmed.

Unrealistic Deadlines

Being able to predict how long something will take is empowering; it will take you far in endearing yourself to those who are depending on you to produce work in a certain time frame. It will make you look organized and in control. But that requires that you can estimate how long something will take and that you avoid, rather than agree to, deadlines that just can't possibly be met. Sometimes you might be tempted agree just to sound as if you're more efficient or to get business that you're afraid you might not get if you say how long it will really take.

You need to also find out if the deadline, however unrealistic, is so crucial that it might be worth it to hire additional staff, even if it's temporary, to help you to meet that deadline or if it's better to extend or change the deadline rather than amend the way you're going about meeting that date.

What's important is to establish a pattern of setting and meeting realistic deadlines. Similar to the pacing example that follows, if you occasionally suggest an unrealistic deadline, that's one thing. But if it's a pattern, unless you figure out why you keep doing it and reverse this tendency you will be wasting a lot of time—yours and everyone else's.

Poor Planning

Have you ever tried to do a month's work in a week or, even worse, in a day? What was that like? What could have been a joyful experience probably turned into a nightmare of all-day and all-night marathons and lots of family and friends wondering when, if ever, they're going to see you.

Now, some types of work do require concentrated periods of intense focus, and that's understandable. One of my girlfriends, for example, had a children's book project from a major publisher with a one-month deadline that had no "wiggle room" to it, so she had to put off everything she could till after the project was done. We set up a luncheon for two months after that, and that is just fine. But if every single time I asked her to lunch or vice versa the same thing happened, it would not just strain our friendship but it would send a message of disorganization and poor planning.

It also negates the fact that, in general, we all need a balanced and full life that includes work and relationships, not just working around the clock.

Inadequate Pacing

You need to pace yourself throughout the day (or evening, if you do evening shift work) so you maximize your efficiency.

Those who don't pace themselves in terms of getting breaks during the day and getting enough rest at night, in extreme cases, might find that working too hard kills them. In Japan, they refer to it as *karoshi,* or death by overwork. *Karoshi* occurs when fatigue and chronic overwork lead to high blood pressure and hardening of the arteries, which proves fatal. Sociologist William Cockerham, in his textbook *Medical Sociology,* notes that of the 98 middle-aged male *karoshi* victims from Tokyo whom he studied, 22.4 percent had worked 50 to 59 hours each week, 32.7 percent worked 70 to 99 hours weekly, and 21.4 percent had worked more than 100 hours a week.

If you are taking a long flight, failing to literally pace yourself by walking up and down the aisles periodically can, in rare cases, lead to a possibly life-threatening blood clot.

Lateness

Lateness is a red flag that you need to avoid as much as possible. Whether it's ten minutes, twenty, or longer, it's going to get people annoyed at you. Now I know there are cultural distinctions; twenty minutes in some cultures may not be considered late at all. But you should try to be on time and let the others be the ones who are late.

When you are late, whether it's when you show up for a meeting or with a project, you had better have a really good explanation. Look, life happens. There are legitimate reasons that you are late for a meeting. Your car broke down. You have a sick relative you have to deal with. A death in the family that devastates you.

But if it's chronic lateness, that's another story. If you are chronically late, you are telling people that are you disorganized and out of control. Your self-management needs work.

If you find yourself having issues with lateness on more than an occasional basis, try to figure out what's behind it. Hostility about a person or place you don't want to go to? Are you going to bed too late at night and not getting enough sleep so you're oversleeping? Are you consistently underestimating how long projects will take or relying on others who are making you wait? Even if they are the ones causing the delays, you are responsible for the outcome so you need to deal with it and not look to others for excuses.

Clutter

There have been whole books written on clutter, including the mega-bestseller *The Life-Changing Magic of Tidying Up* by Marie Kondo. This section won't attempt to duplicate an entire book on decluttering. It does offer my own approach and insights into clutter based on my time management research and observations over the years.

There are basically two types of people who create clutter.

- Type 1: Clutter because of not taking the time to deal with papers or "things" as you go along.
- Type 2: Clutter because of emotional attachment to "things."

Obviously if you fall into the first type of clutterer, it's a lot easier to get rid of your clutter. You need to set aside the time to deal with it.

If you find it hard to allocate time for dealing with clutter, ask a family member, friend, or colleague to be your "clutter buddy." If necessary, hire a professional organizer or declutterer to help you.

It might help to take the time to deal with your clutter or, if you're in the Type 2 category, to get help with your clutter issues if you look at the potential consequences of clutter:

1. Clutter makes it harder and more time-consuming to find what you really need.

2. Clutter creates the opposite of a calm and soothing environment. It is chaos and disorder.

3. Clutter makes it harder to have friends or family "drop in" spontaneously because you feel like you have to "clean up" for guests.

4. You may need a bigger office or even a bigger office building or a larger apartment or house than you really need because your unnecessary clutter is taking up valuable space.

5. You never wanted to be such a materialistic person but somehow, with the accumulation of all this clutter, that is what you have become.

6. Having so much clutter is holding you back from moving forward emotionally and professionally.

7. Clutter makes you feel bad about yourself, and because this is one thing you can proactively

change, why not just declutter and change your situation?

8. You can actually hurt yourself if you don't know what is in a pile and you go to find something and a metal tray comes flying out and falls on your toes. (Yes, this happened to me just the other day when I was doing a major clean up job on one of my rooms! The room now looks great and clutter-free, I'm pleased to report, but my toe is black and blue, but recovering.)

Once you decide you are going to deal with your clutter, you will want to do *something* with it. Here are the main ways you can handle clutter:

- Give it away
- Recycle it
- Throw it out
- Store it somewhere including "off-site"
- Rearrange it so it has its proper place
- Sell it

You want to walk into a room, any room, whether it's your office (or cubicle space) at work or your family room or living room at home, and you want to see the tops of counters. You don't want to see lots of papers everywhere or files that have not been put away.

Ask yourself this question about everything in your office or at home: "Do I really need this?" as well as the follow-up question, "If I give this away/recycle/throw this away, what will happen to me? Will I need this item in a month, a year, a decade?"

When it comes to your own or your kid's school work or art work, find a way to store *original* works that can't be retrieved electronically from a search engine.

To declutter your wardrobe, look at everything in your closet and ask yourself this question, "Have I worn it in the last year?" If you haven't worn it because you gained or lost weight, you will have to ask yourself this additional question, "If I was at the weight that I need to be at to wear this item of clothing, would I want to?" Anything that you answer "no" to you should consider donating to Goodwill or another charitable organization.

Ask your family members to ask the same questions about their clothing (and shoes, accessories, belts, or hats and coats) as you clean out your closets and help those who need clothes and can't afford them to discover those items that you donate.

There are many options for *selling* your clutter if there is clutter that has resale value such as clothing, knick knacks, furniture, books, artwork, equipment in working condition, and memorabilia that others might value but no longer has meaning to you. You could have a tag sale at your home or participate in a neighborhood or group tag sale event. (Be careful about selling directly through a tag sale at your home. You have to be concerned about parking, where you will position your clutter for sale, potential traffic jams if you have a big turnout to your tag sale.)

You can sell your clutter online if you are accepted as a vendor at one of the stores. You can also sell through sites like Craigslist, but once again be careful about personal safety, avoiding allowing total strangers to meet you at your apartment or home to make the sale.

Clutter is not just physical clutter. You might have a cluttered hard drive that is making it hard to find the files that you need. You might own a dozen or more extra domain names that you no longer need to keep renewing that make it harder to focus on the domain names that are important to your business or are costing you a lot more in maintenance fees if you add up what you're spending every year.

If your clutter is papers and you already have one or more filing cabinets at home or at work to store your papers, consider scanning some or all of those papers and storing the papers electronically. If you pick out the key papers that you also need hard copies or the originals, you could consider storing those key files off-site. But be careful about the charges you may incur in storing off-site. I interviewed a woman who put all the furniture and other items from her late mother's home into an off-site storage unit to avoid having it clutter her own apartment. She planned to go through the storage unit and donate or sell everything so she could stop paying for the storage unit. When I interviewed her, she had put off doing that task for a decade, incurring monthly fees and expenses that she realized could be well spent in other ways. So storing off-site is an example of the maxim, "Out of sight, out of mind," but in that case, it was also "out of pocket." So if you do store off-site, especially if it's a temporary measure to deal with your on-site clutter, give yourself some real deadlines for going through the stored materials, hopefully finding a way to permanently get rid of the clutter so you don't have excessive fees.

If you're just using an off-site situation for key original documents, consider renting a safe deposit box at a bank.

Many banks will give you a free safe deposit box as part of a new account that you open or an added benefit to one of the accounts that you already have there. Just make sure you have the names of any beneficiaries or executors of your estate on the safe deposit box or find out the rules at your bank in case you need someone besides yourself to be able to open that box and retrieve its contents.

It might help to make a commitment to one of the junk removal services as a way of dealing with your clutter. If you set up an appointment in a few days or even in a week, that could give you a goal to get some of the clutter organized so you can throw out what can't be donated, recycled, or sold. (Check with the junk removal service if they have the ability to separate your junk into "throw out" and "recycle" piles.)

Check if your town or city has a recycle center where you can bring various items to help you in your declutter efforts. If you get the schedule for the recycling center and make a commitment to take your clutter there—on a specific date, writing that appointment into your appointment book or entering it into your smartphone electronically—that will help you to actually move forward on your decluttering plans.

If you or a family member are Type 2—the emotional clutterer—you have a lot more work to do than the person who creates and fails to deal with clutter because of lack of time to focus on it.

You need to do some "self-talk" about why you hoard things and hold on to things. If self-talk is not enough to cure you, you should consider working with a professional declutterer who has training in helping those with emotional issues related to clutter or a professional therapist, psychiatrist, or psychologist who can help you understand and overcome your clutter issues.

Holding on to the past through the clutter is an obvious reason behind the Type 2 clutterer. But, unfortunately, it's not all that simple to stop doing it. The emotional routes behind being a clutterer need to be addressed or there can be a severe emotional reaction to cold turkey taking away the clutter just like with the cold turkey stopping of any addiction. So if you fall into the Type 2 category, don't be shy about asking for help. Fortunately, there *is* help available. There is also nothing to be ashamed of if you have become a clutterer and you are in need of help.

Now that we've explored how you can gain better control over yourself, including how to overcome 22 time wasters, in the next chapter we will look at two pivotal issues for improving your time management—office relationships and figuring out what is expected of you at work.

Chapter 6

Office Relationships
and Expectations

Spending the time to get along with others at work or in business is not an "extra" that you get to when you're done with your work. It is an integral part of your work.

If you work in an office, or if you are performing any kind of job, you have to be concerned about the people you are working with, not just the actual job you're doing. An executive with a nice long track record of jobs in traditional offices—more than a decade at one company and more than a decade at another major one—says, "When you work in an office, half your time you spend doing your job and the other half of the time you spend making sure you don't lose your job."

5 Principles to Build Strong Work Relationships

One of my favorite quotes about the importance of work relationships is from an interview I did with public relations executive Harold Burson of Burson-Marstellar. As Harold Burson, co-founder of public relations giant Burson-Marsteller, said to me, "People get promoted as much with the approval of the people they work with as the people who are their bosses.") (Quoted in my book *Friendshifts*, Chapter 11, and "How Friendship Enhances Your Career.")

Unfortunately, too many fail to realize how pivotal co-workers are in their effectiveness at a company until the damage has been done and getting their relationships and their job back on track can't be undone. Take the time now to assess your relationships at work so you don't fall into that trap!

Here are five principles that will help you to get along better at work and in business, which will increase your productivity:

1. Practice business protocol in every interaction. Researchers have found that if someone is pleased with your service, they will tell one person; if displeased, they will tell five or more about their disappointment.

2. Take the time to connect with others through what's similar about you rather than focusing on your differences.

3. Respect that everyone has a special comfort level for intimacy and personal space. Friendship takes time and sometimes it complicates the workplace or business connections more than it helps it, so at least initially, until trust is earned, aim instead for what I call a *workship*—a work relationship that is more than an acquaintance but less intimate (or demanding) than a friendship.

4. Don't put in writing—and that includes posts on social media sites including Facebook.com, LinkedIn.com, or Twitter.com—anything that you don't want to see published on the front page of a newspaper or on the Internet. Be careful what you say about others. Even sharing praise or good news about others, if it's inappropriate or premature, can backfire.

5. Referrals are a great way to grow your business, so put time and effort into each business relationship; a satisfied client is your best advertisement. Go the distance with each client, customer, co-worker, boss, employee, or service provider.

Partnerships Can Save You Time but Be Careful You Pick the Right One

Ben Cohen and Jerry Greenfield co-founded Ben & Jerry's, an enormously popular ice cream company. Two brothers, Richard and Maurice McDonald, co-founded the McDonald's hamburger operation in 1948. In 1938, Bill Hewlett and David Packard co-founded the company that would become computer giant Hewlett-Packard. Larry Page and Sergey Brin co-founded Google.com in 1998.

Yes, partnerships can have amazing positive business outcomes. Working with a partner might be a productive step for you and your company. But it might backfire and lead to weeks, months, or years of non-productive effort as well as bad feelings and, in some extreme cases, lawsuits or worse.

How do you know if a partnership is going to work out? Here are some questions to ask yourself if you're considering this option:

- Do your personalities compliment, compete, or conflict with each other?

- Do you share the same values, or is there a value clash?

- Is your response time similar, or is one of you prone to move projects along and the other one has a more laid back approach?

- Do your skills and capabilities compliment, duplicate, or compete with each other?

- Will your communication styles work well together?

- Is the person you're considering as a partner psychologically healthy?

- Do you like each other?

- Can you see yourself spending long stretches of time together?

There are no right or wrong answers to the above questions just as there are no partnerships that are guaranteed to work out or those that are doomed to failure. My observation, however, is that if you start off with two people who are psychologically healthy and if each one of you has a unique skill set so that you are more likely to complement rather than compete with each other, it might have a better chance at succeeding than if you are clashing over everything, including who gets the most attention or whose opinion will have the most weight.

For example, if you complement each other, one of you may be good at numbers and the other is the creative one, or one of you is going to do the marketing and public speaking to get the word out about your product and the other is going to be doing the product development.

If a partnership is producing the financial rewards that your company needs, for some the answer is selling to someone else. That's what the McDonald brothers did when, in 1954, they sold their chain of 21 burger stores to Ray Kroc from Illinois who bought the restaurants and name rights for $2.7 million; today, current annual sales estimates for the global empire are in the billions.

Bringing in another partner to help with the skills that you lack or to create a new dynamic might be another answer if your partnership is floundering. It will now be a company split three ways, or you and your partner could have your new partner have a smaller stake in the company but he or she could offer skills that you need. It will probably be easier to fix a partnership where the issues are business-related rather than if there is a personality clash that just doesn't seem to resolve itself amicably.

Figuring Out What You Need to Do versus What Others Expect You to Do

When I do time management workshops, the concept that causes more attendees to take a deep breath or grasp is when I say, "It's not what you're procrastinating about that will cause the most problems in your job or career. At least you know you're putting something off. It's the things you should be doing that you're not even aware that you need to do—it's not

even on your radar screen—that's what's going to derail you."
What are some examples of this in a variety of professions?

- Publishers who refused to accept that e-books were not just "coming" at some point but were actually already transforming the way information (books) are being delivered.

- Musicians who cling to the old style of performing, or selling, their music.

- Celebrities who are trying to grow their fan base the old-fashioned way without a concern for Twitter and online communities.

- Travel agents who haven't factored in hotels.com, trivago.com, or expedia.com as competition.

Here's an anecdote from my own life that applies to the idea that you should make sure you are doing what you need to be doing in the first place.

I had some time before I started graduate work in art therapy, so I took a job for a couple of months at a jewelry manufacturing company in Philadelphia. I was in the office doing billings and answering the phone, and the office was this small, glass-enclosed space that looked out on to the jewelry makers, the minimum wage workers who were putting the earrings together.

The company had hundreds of different earrings and there was no catalogue for what the company offered. Each order was just fulfilled as it came in.

I had majored in art and I loved to draw, so I decided to make a catalogue of the earrings, drawing a picture of each available design and writing a short description.

The catalogue was a work of art and, I believed, so very useful to the company.

I shared the prototype of what I had done with my boss, and he was not at all impressed. He basically said—I'm paraphrasing but this was the concept behind his harsh words—"We don't need a catalogue. If we needed one, we'd have one."

I had been working on the catalogue in my spare time, not during the day when I would answer the phone or do the paperwork, so it wasn't a question of wasting the company's time. But I had certainly wasted mine. Not only didn't I get the praise or a bonus or a promotion, but I got yelled at!

That experience at the age of 21 helped me to try, in the future, to find out just what the person I worked for needed and wanted rather than doing what I thought should be done and, in the process, wasting time I could have used in a much more productive way.

One of the biggest challenges for anyone who wants to achieve success in business and to be more productive in our career is to know what we need to do versus what others tell us to do. How many of us have learned this the hard way as well? You get hired by someone to do a specific job, but then, instead of being given *carte blanche* to do that job, you are told that there is another priority or two that you need to do first or at the same time.

Here is the dilemma: if you don't do the second job, which office politics requires that you also perform, you will be seen as insubordinate. But if you fail to make the time to do the job that you were initially hired to do, you will, in the long run, be sabotaging yourself.

So all of us usually have at least two, possibly three or more jobs:

1.   The job you're hired to do

2.   The job you're told you have to do (which might not be the same as number one)

3.   The integration of both of those priorities into your workday

In the next chapter we'll look at making your office space more effective as well as getting more out of meeings.

Office Efficiency and Making Your Office Space Work Better for You

Here are some rules for enhanced office efficiency that apply whether you are an optician who see clients you fit for eyeglasses or an office worker who types on a computer in a cubicle each day:

1. Separate active and inactive materials or even files and have what you need all the time handy and put the rest away.

2. File when something happens rather than putting it off and letting it pile up. That could mean entering the business cards of those you meet at a conference into a database that night or putting the clippings from research you have accumulated into the correct files. This could refer to physical or electronic filing or sorting.

3. Back up what you do.

4.   Look over your office and consider how you can rearrange the furniture for enhanced productivity.

Becoming More Productive at Your Job

The Goal, written by Dr. Eli Goldratt with Jeff Cox, is an extremely influential business and time management book that is written as a fable or parable. It uses the story of Alex Rogo and his quest to save his plant from closing in three months to teach readers about how a factory can become more productive. The specifics are somewhat technical, geared more to manufacturing than to typical office situations, but the broader lessons are very pertinent. If any of us want to be more productive, we must ask and answer these three questions:

- What to change?
- What to change to?
- How to cause the change?

Dr. Goldratt offers sage advice to Rogo through an Israeli management consultant named Jonah who appears throughout *The Goal* from time to time, always flying in from exciting places around the world, like Singapore. He implements his suggestions at the plant leading to greater productivity; a closure is avoided.

Let's apply Dr. Goldratt's questions to your own situation:

1. What do you want to change?

_____

_____

_____

2.   What do you want to change that situation to?

_____

_____

_____

3.   What are you going to do to make the change
happen? What steps are you going to take to accomplish 1 and 2?

_____

_____

_____

Making Your Space More Effective

I wrote an entire book on this topic entitled *Making Your
Office Work for You* in which I cover everything from the
color of your walls to what's hanging on your walls, your type
of office, office furniture, and placement of that furniture.
Here are some of the key ideas in that book that you might
find useful:

- You may spend as much or even more time in
  your office than you will spend at home. You
  take time to consider the furnishings in your
  apartment or home, don't you? So take the time
  to consider your office.

- You may feel that you don't have any control
  over what furniture you have in your office,
  especially if you work for someone else. But at
  least consider the chair that you sit on. If the
  chair you use is not an ergonomic chair which

will increase your efficiency and decrease the likelihood of backaches, see if you could purchase such a chair on your own as the cost has become much more affordable. (And you and/or your company will probably more than make up the cost of the chair in increased productivity and reduced discomfort caused by aches.)

- Consider the position of your office. If you have a job that relies on interaction with others, you might want to be closer to other offices. If your job requires more concentration and working on your own, being away from others might work better.

- When I was researching my book, I interviewed a woman who had a very messy office. She apologized and told me that she'd get around to cleaning up her office after she got her real work done. But having an efficient workspace that maximizes your productivity *is* part of your real work. Just as you would tidy up your living room if you knew you were having visitors over, you want to keep your office as neat as possible, sending a message to you and to your coworkers and to management that you are in control of your workspace.

- Have a sweater or jacket available in case the office gets too cold or lighter clothes to switch to if it gets too hot, especially if someone else is in control of the office temperature.

- Choose what is on your desk as well as what is on your walls to maximize your efficiency but also with an eye to the impression you want to make on others. As sociologist Erving Goffman discussed in his classic works, we need to be aware of "information management" about ourselves as well as about our *Presentation of Self in Everyday Life,* the title of one of his landmark books.

Making the Most of Meetings

Meetings are part and parcel of the work that most of us do, whether those meetings take place in person, at an outside office, at a coffee shop, or if we work at home and prefer to have our meetings in a public space or at a booth or a stand if the meeting takes place at a trade show around the corner or in another part of the world.

Meetings can be exciting as well as a very productive way to find out what's going on with others at your company. You may also learn the trends and developments in a field if you meet with others from companies in another part of your country or of the globe.

Poor planning and preparation is probably one of the biggest ways that meetings are less productive than a meeting could be as well as the over-scheduling that was addressed in Chapter 5, one of the time wasters discussed under Logistics. So let's look at the other ways that you could improve on the outcome of your meeting by applying time management principles to each and every meeting.

First of all, for each meeting, set a goal.

Every single meeting should have a specific goal for that interaction, not a general goal for all your meetings.

Create a plan in advance of what you want to do at the meeting. What will you discuss? Have talking points prepared.

Prioritize what you have to do.

If you're trying to sell something during your meeting, make sure you leave enough time for your pitch and to close the deal. If you spend almost all your meeting time chatting about more general matters, you might not get to your main goal of selling.

Pace yourself.

In addition to avoiding over-scheduling, you want to have time between meetings so that you have free time so you can relax. If your meetings are not nearby, make sure you allow enough time for travel.

Be self-directing.

Yes, it's fine to accept invitations to meet from those who ask you for a meeting and you want to take that meeting. But also take the time to proactively reach out to others, whether you meet through a referral or a social media initial contact.

Find a mentor.

Do you know someone who is excellent at one-on-one meetings? Take a meeting with that individual and ask him or her to mentor you so you can improve your own meeting skills.

Reward yourself and the person with whom you met for having your meeting.

The reward could be a simple e-mail "thank you" or a handwritten note that you send. Or you might even pick up the phone and say thank you for the meeting.

You can apply the same seven principles of basic time management to the meetings that you attend at your company, whether that meeting is with your boss or with your department. In that way, you will increase what you bring to, and what you get out of, each and every meeting. Those meetings will become tools to enhance your productivity instead of the time-wasting events that so many, unfortunately, see most one-on-one or group meetings to be.

In the next chapter, we will look at the growing trend toward fragmentation and how to reverse that trend so that you are more focused and productive.

Chapter 8

Overcoming Fragmentation

There will be interruptions to your day. It will be hard for most of us to find 30 minutes, an hour, or more of quiet, seamless time. And that's just the reality of work today. But if you can stop the self-interruptions that are behind most fragmentation, you are more likely to have at least some time to concentrate, meditate, or be focused on one priority task.

How do you avoid having your day chopped up into 1,440 minutes? How do you get back to the quality and focused time that will lead to greater creativity, innovation, and productivity?

In my book *Work Less, Do More*, I contributed the term "distractionitis." Just what is distractionitis? Here are some questions to ask yourself to know if you are suffering from it:

- Do you check e-mail every few minutes throughout the day?

- Do you let your mobile phone go to voice mail or grab every call even if you're in an important meeting?

- Do you read or send text messages whenever the opportunity presents itself?

These are just some of the many examples of distractionitis.

Now, however, I see the trend toward distractionitis growing to the point that it has become a major anti-productivity development that I refer to as *fragmentation*. Fragmentation can be defined as the erosion of calm, quality time to think, the evaporation of the minutes or hours from a day that could lead to breakthrough thinking and innovation.

Getting More Focused in a 24/7 World

Years ago I took a course in transcendental meditation. I picked a word that would be my mantra—I still remember what it is after all these years—and it taught me to take time each day to meditate.

It was suggested that I spend twenty minutes a day meditating; today, at the website for transcendental meditation, it is still recommended that you take 15 to 20 minutes a day to meditate.

Transcendental meditation is one way to reclaim your inner calm, to reverse the trend toward fragmentation. But there are other ways that may work for you. Look around your office. What distractions do you see that may prevent you from being focused and concentrating? Do you stare out the window in an unproductive way? For you, taking the time and spending the money to install blinds or to put up curtains that you close for even part of the day might be an answer.

Do you have a radio on that is distracting you, or, by contrast, is there so much commotion from those who work around you or nearby that having a radio and playing soothing background music might help you to focus? (You might need to use earphones.)

Is your chair comfortable, or do you need an ergonomic chair that will make it better for you to sit at your desk for long periods? You can purchase an ergonomic chair for a fraction of what such a chair used to cost; it could be an excellent investment for you and for your company in terms of a return on the investment because of your enhanced productivity.

The biggest source of fragmentation today, however, is not even because of structural causes but because of too many of us trying to work on too many projects at once.

ADHD (Attention Deficit Hyperactivity Disorder)

For some, fragmentation is part of their approach to the world. Those individuals have been diagnosed as children, teens, or even as adults as someone who has ADHD, which stands for Attention Deficit Hyperactivity Disorder. Here are the key characteristics of those with ADHD:

- Inattention
- Hyperactivity
- Impulsivity

You might consider seeing a physician and getting an accurate diagnosis if your inattention is interfering with your ability to do your job and to stay focused. If you do have ADHD, it's possible that medication might be helpful to you.

ADT (Attention Deficit Trait)

This is a condition that was named by psychiatrist Edward M. Hallowell, who is also the founder of the Hallowell Centers for Cognitive and Emotional Health. In his article "Overloaded Circuits," Hallowell defines ADT, a term he invented, as the condition with these key symptoms: "distractibility, inner frenzy, and impatience."

Raise your hand if that describes you, at least now. How many of us would raise our hands!

What is the cause of ADT, according to Dr. Hallowell? "Brain overload." I see it caused by "doing too much at once," which leads to brain overload because the brain can only focus on so many projects, concerns, clients, or patients at once before you get ADT, brain overload, or the feeling of being frenzied and out of control of your life.

Here are Hallowell's three suggestions for controlling ADT:

1. Foster positive emotions.

2. Take physical care of your brain.

3. Organize for ADT.

Hallowell says that by connecting face to face with people throughout your day, you will foster positive emotions. I also suggest that those people, as much as possible, are positive people who make you feel inspired, motivated, and uplifted rather than downtrodden and sad.

If you work alone, or at home, you can still make sure you interact face to face for some or part of the day by going out to lunch, rather than bringing lunch from home, taking a walk during lunch time, or taking a short break and walking over to a store, a workout center, or a library where you could chat with other patrons or even ask a question of someone working at the desk.

If you are single and unattached and you work alone, in addition to trying to have face-to-face contact at some point during the day, consider building face-to-face interaction into your evenings. Whether that means you work out at a health club, make a commitment to ongoing volunteer work, or become part of activities related to your interests, you want to try to avoid spending your day working all alone and then also being alone throughout the evening.

People offer us a chance to have someone to bounce our ideas off of as well as someone to share our daily triumphs and challenges with. If you live with someone, whether it's a romantic partner or family members, sometimes we all need to be reminded to reach out to those you see every day and might even be taking for granted. Don't wait to be asked about how your day went. If necessary, volunteer some information and, if possible, end by asking, "And how was your day?" and mean it, really mean it, as you listen and respond to what you're hearing.

The advice Hallowell shares for taking care of your brain you've heard before, but it bears repeating—get the sleep you need, eat healthy, and exercise on a regular basis.

Finally, Hallowell's suggestions for "organizing for ADT" include keeping part of your desk clear "at all times" as well as denoting part of your day for "thinking and planning." Take note of the suggestions I offered in Chapter 7, in the section on office efficiency, about how to make your office more effective that could be useful to you in carrying out this "organizing for ADT" suggestion.

More Tips for Dealing with Fragmentation

There are some, however, for whom fragmentation is just part of how they approach every day. I used to be like that till I found that by forcing myself to tackle and finish one major project at a time, I could accomplish more and feel less fragmented and discombobulated than giving in to the fragmentation. I still, however, "self-fragment" my time by checking e-mails far more frequently than I should, although I am working on overcoming that unproductive habit. For those in that category, it's necessary for you to find a way to work around your tendency and to find a way to make your need to be involved in multiple projects work for you. I personally and professionally tried that, and for me it led to burnout, frustration, and overeating.

Since I have cut back on the number of things I do at once, I feel less fragmented. I'm working more methodically, one project at a time, the way I used to work in "the old days," and I seem to be getting the total number of projects done in the same amount of time, just without as much frenzy and in a much more cohesive way. The key is that it takes saying "no" to more people and letting others know what your priorities are, which can be a bit daunting and scary if you've fallen into the habit of saying "yes" to everyone, trying to do everything at once, only to find that you're overwhelmed and also disappointed at the quality as well as the quantity of your accomplishments.

Telling others that they will have to wait for you to get to their demand on you till you can get to it requires trust in each other that you're not going to push away that additional project indefinitely. You also need a shared agreement that just because something is being finished first does not mean that next project, or the second or third one after that, is not a priority as well. You just have to make the difficult judgment call about what will be finished first, a decision that might be coming from way above or based on whether something is a seasonal project with a specific deadline, or a whole multitude of factors.

Here's how time management skills and a commitment to dealing with fragmentation can help you with a major task that you need to do. Let's take, as an example, writing my last major book before this one. That book, entitled *The Fast Track Guide to Speaking in Public*, had a specific deadline. Yes, it's true that I had been speaking for decades and I even taught a course related to the book, but I had not yet written the actual book. I had a table of contents and about 5,000 words, but that was just a start to the book.

Now "all" I had to do was write a book including getting additional interviews and research that I thought necessary. I had a firm commitment for that book on speaking, and I didn't want to disappoint my editor. Instead of finding a million excuses for putting off writing that book, I decided that two weeks was a realistic time frame to get a complete draft written and to the proofreader.

I had to say "no" to lots of distractions over those two weeks. It helped to put into my appointment book, at the beginning of each day, across the top of the book that I was working on that project. It made it concrete. It was there for me to look at and remember as my priority concern for each day.

Voila, I finished, and I was truly exhausted. While the book was at the proofreader, I cleaned up my office since so many files had been pulled out to help me in my writing. I was catching my breath. Although I was pleased that I had finally finished that book project, I promised myself to try to pace myself better the next time because the intensity was extreme. The good news, however, is that it was a short-term intensity. Many of us have such intermittent deadlines and we do, on occasion, have to pull away from the world, or at least let those we care about know that for a few hours or days or even weeks we need to be focused with laser sharp intensity on a priority project.

The problem today, however, is that too many are finding instead of being in that type of an intense situation for a couple of hours, days, or weeks, it's become months and even years. But the way that I was able to write a book—based on an area of expertise I already had, I might add—in just two weeks is by avoiding the fragmentation that so many of us have found eating away at our productivity.

If I could avoid fragmentation and accomplish so much in just two weeks, you can do it too! And if we apply the same laser sharp focus to what we set out to do each and every day, avoiding the wasted time from mindlessly surfing the net or switching back and forth between checking e-mails and doing the "real work," imagine what heights we could all reach and in a less frenzied and overwrought way.

Using the P.I.E. Technique: Prioritize, Initiate, Evaluate

Scheduling one's life effectively also allows one to be involved in activities that would have otherwise been left out of it. By allowing some special time for certain activities, the schedule makes sure that we get to do them.

—SOCIOLOGIST EVIATAR ZERUBAVEL,
Hidden Rhythms

The reason I developed the concept of the P.I.E. approach to a day and evening is that I realized that my own situation of juggling multiple jobs and roles is actually not all that unique these days. The CEO I mentioned in the very beginning of this book—in addition to his main job and being a husband, father of three, and son—is in charge of a major annual community event. My own P.I.E. is divided up in this way—writing books, articles, and occasional blogs; being an adjunct assistant professor at a college; coaching; speaking professionally; being an entrepreneur who runs a small press; as well as my personal and professional obligations as a wife, mother, grandmother, extended family member, friend, and colleague. I may not work on each of those roles daily, and some roles are seasonal, such as being a college professor during the fall and spring semesters, but unless I do something related to each of those roles at some point during the week, month, or year, my productivity will decline.

Nina Roesner is an Ohio-based 49-year-old whose P.I.E. is divided up in this way—she is a homeschool mom, the executive director of an international non-profit organization called Greater Impact, an author, a teacher at college, as well as a teacher of courses for her non-profit.

You might find it helpful to see your career (and day and evening) visually as part of a "pie." You can divide the pie up into hours or into tasks or roles that you have to fulfill.

Most of us would love to have all our hours to devote to one task and, once that task is done, to then move on to the next one. In reality, we all have to give some time to this priority task and some time to another. We need to address each of our priority tasks until each task is completed.

If your work environment enables you to do just one thing till it's completed, aren't you the lucky one. But most are more likely to be in work situations similar to what my college students are dealing with, juggling five courses a semester. Some even have a part-time or a full-time job, and others also have family obligations that they have to deal with.

For them, a P.I.E. approach with a certain number of minutes or hours each day or every other day devoted to each of the courses that they are studying will help them to achieve good grades in all their courses. If they favor only one or two courses, unfortunately that will probably be reflected in how much they learn and in their grades.

In the workplace, it's often harder to see the tasks that we are being asked to do as clearly as it is to see the courses you are taking when you're in high school, college, or graduate school. But there are still clear and specific tasks or projects that we have to do. The difference is that, usually, we are the ones who need to set the deadlines, monitor our progress, and make sure that everything that we need to do gets done. Everyone needs to work hard to make sure that nothing slips through the cracks.

In addition to the concept of the pie is the acronym that PIE stands for:

P = prioritize

I = initiate

E = evaluate

P = prioritize

Make sure each task you are doing is a priority for you.

I = initiate

Get going on each task that you have to do each day, even each hour. Avoid procrastination or you will sabotage yourself. If you are procrastinating, figure out why, and focus on getting back on track and on task as soon as possible.

E = evaluate

None of us work or live in a vacuum. We all need to keep evaluating our priorities and our goals and how we are spending our time. If your job changes, if you finish a project and need to go on to the next project, you need to evaluate how your P.I.E. should be divided up and what is in it.

There are lots of ways to view the P.I.E. technique. You could make your entire day one pie, as in the first sample below. This is what the day and evening of someone who has to make a lot of sales calls might look like. It's not looking at the day by hours but by tasks. There are two slots for commuting because there is the morning and end of day commuting. There should be time for lunch, so there is a small lunch slot. There is time for sleep and for dinner.

If it's useful, consider using colored highlighters or markets to distinguish each piece of each day's P.I.E.

P.I.E. Sample #1

In addition to this visual P.I.E. reminder of all the tasks this salesperson has to do, she or he might want to use a *Daily Time Log* to make sure that each task is being accomplished. Or even block out time in an electronic or paper daily appointment book. I personally like the DayMinder® 8½ x 11 weekly professional appointment book created by AACO Brands out of Dayton, Ohio because it starts at 7 in the morning and it goes to 9:45 at night. There is a line and slot for every 15 minutes during the day up till 9:45 P.M., Monday through Friday. For Saturday, it ends at 6:45 P.M. instead, and for Sunday there is a smaller space and it is a blank area, without any specific times at all. I have tried using electronic appointment systems and it simply does not work as well for me as an old-fashioned paper one. But you might find an electronic calendar or even a scheduling app works well for you rather than a paper one.

What system do you use? If it's helping you to be efficient, that's great. If not, try another system, paper or electronic, till you find one that is ideal for you now—not yesterday or tomorrow, but now.

P.I.E. Sample #2

For the second P.I.E. approach, (illustrated above) each of the sections of the P.I.E.s represents an hour for one day. So put into each of those hours what you will be doing or, if you want to use this system retrospectively to get a better understanding of how you spent your time, insert what you did during that hour.

A third type of P.I.E., illustrated next, shows two P.I.E.s, one for A.M. and the other for the P.M. hours. Use this version to track your activities.

P.I.E. Sample #3

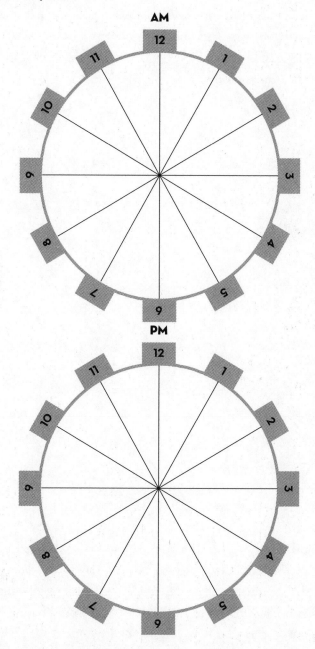

The goal of the P.I.E. system is to give you a much better understanding of where your time is going, what you are doing with your time, and how it is being spent, not wasted. If it is being wasted, you will see how to stop wasting it and start using it in a more productive way.

P.I.E. Sample #4

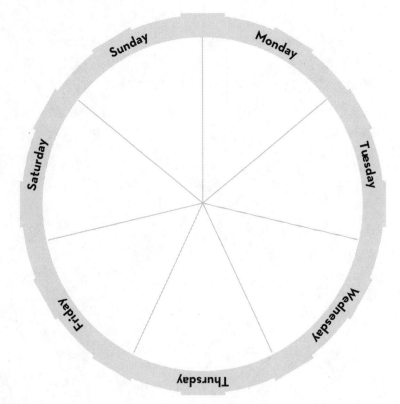

Another way to use the P.I.E. approach (illustrated above) is to think of each piece of your pie as a day in the week. You might devote one complete day to a certain task or job, another day to another, and so on. In that case, you would have a P.I.E. for the week, showing how you planned the focus for each day, and a second P.I.E. (as in samples # 1, 2, or 3) for how you will divide up the hours within each of those days.

An ancillary "system" that will help you to get more done—and, as you may recall, the number one time management tool used by 74 percent of the 127 men and women I surveyed—is a "to do" list (discussed in Chapter 4). Creating and following a to-do list—in addition to your P.I.E. for the day and evening and, if necessary, tracking your time through a Daily Time Log—are productivity skills and techniques that will help you to *Put More Time on Your Side*. (For more on Daily Time Logs, as well as two blank samples, see the Appendix.)

In the Appendix, you will find blank P.I.E.s that you can use to create a visual reminder of what you have to accomplish today and tomorrow.

In the next chapter, we'll explore being or becoming a visionary.

Chapter 10

Being or Becoming a Visionary

Visionaries get what has to get done completed, and in as efficient a way as possible, so they can then spend time on what they know is the next big thing. You need to give yourself the time to ponder what your next big thing should be.

Are you a visionary? Have you been privileged to know visionaries? There are visionaries in every field. My mother was a visionary kindergarten teacher. She wrote songs that her students performed. She created unique ways of teaching the key concepts that kindergarteners need to know. I had a ninth grade social studies teacher, Mr. Smollar. Unfortunately he died of cancer that summer at a relatively young age—he was only in his late 20s—but he left with me a lifelong commitment to a way of teaching that was visionary. When we studied about Africa, you didn't just read a textbook; he taught in a multimedia way so that even before computers or YouTube.com our class was somehow transported to whatever part of the world we were studying.

Stamina

One of the qualities of a visionary is that you don't let adversity stop you. It might slow you down temporarily, but you learn from it and move on. In her *Harvard Business Review* article "How Resilience Works," journalist Diane L. Coutu recalls an example of someone she worked with at a national magazine, someone she calls Claus Schmidt, who had many personal tragedies befall him, but he always rebounded. He survived the purging of staffs at the magazine not just once but three times. She comments on the positive attitude Claus always showed in the newsroom; he did not dwell on the negative.

Claus, according to Coutu, was a resilient person. Resilient people, Coutu notes, have these three traits: "They coolly accept the harsh realities facing them. They find meaning in terrible times. And they have an uncanny ability to improvise, making do with whatever's at hand."

Unfortunately, you can't just say to someone who's miserable or who's just lost his or her job, "Get over it. Find a new job. Turn your sadness into productive activities so you can reach your goal." There is a period of time, which varies with each individual, that someone needs to grieve and to recover from dramatic change, especially sudden and undesirable change such as losing a job or learning that someone you care about is ill or has died. But the sooner someone else—or you—pick yourself up, dust yourself off, and get back into taking on the world and trying to make positive things happen, the more productive and self-satisfied you will be.

Where does that stamina come from? Part of it might be your personality, your DNA. You just were born having more stamina and resilience. But part of it also comes from having inner security, the opposite of the time waster of insecurity, which I addressed in Chapter 5.

How do you develop that inner security? In an ideal world, you would be born to parents who loved you, who believed in you, but who didn't overindulge you or over-praise you so you're afraid to go out into the "real" world to see how your skills or talents will hold up against outside competition.

I hope you had parents like that. Stand up if you did.

What? You're not standing? Or you're half-standing or you want to tell me that perhaps one of your parents was like that, but your other parent was more negative and critical. Or perhaps your parents were loving and approving and motivating, but your siblings were jealous and even cruel to you, belittling you and hurting your self-esteem.

You cannot rewrite your past. None of us can do that. What happened occurred and it is what it is. But you can decide, today, at this very moment, that you will not let your past, and whatever emotional residue you have suffered from it, stop you from being the most focused, efficient, productive, happy, and successful person that you can be.

You can give to yourself the security that others either failed to give to you or that, even if they tried to give it to you, for whatever reason you were not ready to receive it from them at that time.

But now you are. You are ready to receive it from yourself. You will that inner security to yourself that will lead to you being a more resilient person with more stamina.

You can get in touch with the inner strength and courage that you have to be the best you can be. The best car salesman. The best mutual fund manager. The best writer. The best speaker. The best parent. The best husband. The best wife. The best citizen. The best teacher. The best whatever you are or want to be.

We all have a personality that is who we are—our very own unique way of being—and that can be the secure you, the triumphant you. You might find reading the stories of those who faced adversity but survived it inspirational. Decades ago I somehow stumbled on the memoir of Viktor E. Frankl, a psychiatrist who was in a concentration camp in the 1940s and who survived. All of his family perished except one sister who had escaped Austria and went to Australia, and she found his description of what he went through, and how he survived it, riveting. Frankl died at the age of 92 in 1997, but his book, under the English title of *A Man's Search for Meaning*, is still a bestseller.

Not only are Frankl's words and insights beautifully written and insightful, but writing it down was a way of working through that horrific experience and providing the rest of us with what he went through, and learned, through his eyes.

Another memoir that you may not have heard of written by a woman who was in a concentration camp when she was a young child is called *Forbidden Strawberries* by Cipora Hurwitz. Hurwitz's story is another page turner of a memoir that is evidence of the power of writing and of surviving the toughest of situations.

On the Road to Being a Visionary

Steve Jobs of Apple was a visionary. There are many who see the contribution of Jobs as equaled by few. PR giant Harold Burson wrote in one of his blogs that he thinks the only other business leaders to change lives to the extent that Jobs did in the last 150 years were Thomas Edison and Henry Ford.

Whether or not you agree with Jobs' stature as an inventor, he certainly changed the way millions upon millions of us around the world interact and do business as well as how we keep up with our families. I heard several interviews with Jobs in which journalists asked him how he came up with the ideas for the Apple products. He often was even asked if he did focus groups or market research to find out what people needed.

But Jobs explained that his process was a bit different. I'm paraphrasing what he answered, but the gist of it is that he created products that no one knew they needed until he had created them. That's why he couldn't ask consumers what they'd like him to create because his products were so revolutionary—and he was such a visionary—that they didn't even know what it could do, so how could they ask for it?

I have an iPhone and I know that I initially resisted buying one, even though my sister Eileen kept telling me that it would help my business and change my life. But I didn't have one yet and I hadn't yet seen its capabilities, so I couldn't understand just what all the fuss was about.

Then one day, I went to an appointment at a TV studio in Manhattan. I had traveled all the way from my home in Connecticut, which took over two hours. When I left that morning for the meeting, everything was in place. The meeting had been confirmed the day before. But when I arrived at the meeting, I was told that the person I was meeting with had sent me an e-mail to explain that she had to change our meeting.

At that point, I only had a cell phone. I didn't have a smartphone with e-mail capability. So I never got the e-mail because it had been sent to my computer, which was back home in Connecticut.

Fortunately, we worked out that if I was willing to wait an hour or two, she would arrive and we could finally have our meeting. But that experience was just the last straw in many communications I was missing out on by failing to have portable e-mail capability, so I marched over to an AT&T store when I got home later that day and signed up for my iPhone.

At first, I just used the iPhone for phone calls and e-mails. But then I started using it to take photos as well as video that I used in business. When I met with someone at a conference, I would immediately put their information in my contact part of the phone, and I would sometimes add their picture to the contact information so I had a better likelihood of remembering them when we communicated by e-mail afterward or met at the next conference a year or two later.

I can't even begin to count all the meetings that have been changed, rescheduled, or even made in the first place because I have a smartphone, increasing my efficiency by leaps and bounds.

Thank you Steve Jobs and Apple.

There are, of course, now lots of competitive and equally useful smartphones to choose from, but it was the Apple iPhone and the vision of Steve Jobs and his company that have led the way. Ditto for the iPad, which is transforming the way that so many companies handle paper or even have eliminated needing it. Some may say that's a bad thing, but that's another issue. The productivity benefits and the value of being a visionary are what's under discussion here.

What does it mean to be a visionary in your field? It could be something like finding a way to make your office more efficient by rearranging the furniture or restructuring the day so that everyone gets a twenty-minute exercise break to help improve health by pacing better and getting up out of a chair. Or, if your job requires that you stand most of the day, giving you time to sit down.

Connecting to Movers and Shakers

How do you connect to the movers and shakers who will catapult you to the top of your career? The first step is identifying who those individuals are whom you want to meet.

The next step is figuring out where they hang out, whether it's in person or online. What social media are they connected to that might make you that much closer to connecting? Will Linkedin.com be your way to get to him or her? That's a growing trend, as you probably know. It has grown from a company that began with five co-founders in the living room of the co-founder, Reid Hoffman, in 2002 to a professional network in more than 195 countries with more than 450 million users globally.

What conferences does he or she attend? Even better, where is this individual speaking because that might give you an opportunity to go up to him or her afterward, introduce yourself, offer your business card, get his or her business card in exchange, and possibly start a business connection from that point on.

Of course, the more high profile the mover and shaker you want to connect to, and the more that individual has a celebrity status, the more likely access will be denied to you, including the presence of security guards, without having a proper introduction in advance. So for some movers and shakers, the best way to initiate a relationship is through the introduction by a trusted friend, family member, or colleague. Even once the introduction is made, you have to respond to each other in an equally positive way that you both want to continue and cultivate your interaction.

Access is the first step. A shared wish to connect and cultivate a relationship is the next step. It's very much like what you need for a friendship to ensue, just on a professional and business basis.

Sometimes a mover and shaker will reach out to you and you might not even be aware of it because the time waster of insecurity distorts the way you're viewing the situation. Instead of seeing the overture as genuine and sincere and an opportunity, you see it as an artificial gesture that you ignore. Sadly, that leads to a missed opportunity!

So you need to work on overcoming the time waster of insecurity so you can be more realistic in how you see the WOOs in your life. (You will learn more about WOOs—*windows of opportunity*—in chapter 13 of this book.)

Taking a trip together is another way to consider connecting to movers and shakers. Yes, it can be a big investment of time and money. But to get the best chance of making those connections, the further away, the more exotic, and the more unique the experience, the more likely the connection might occur. Not only will you have the time and opportunity to interact, but you will always have those shared memories of the trip to help you bond more.

The concept behind this strategy is to find out what conferences the movers and shakers you want to meet are attending, and also if there are side trips sponsored by the association before or after the conference and who is going on those side trips. This information may be listed at the website for the association and the conference.

You can, of course, on your own go on exotic, exciting, and meaningful trips, such as volunteering for a good cause in other parts of the world or a business summit organized by a chamber of commerce, but you might not meet the movers and shakers you are seeking to befriend.

More Effective Relationships

How do you connect to your children, your spouse, your friends, or your boss so you embrace each day in the most productive way possible? Do you take the time, not just during the holidays or for someone's birthday, to say, "I appreciate you," "I like you," or "I love you"?

Showing and saying you care about someone is a form of reward. It's not materialistic, like a new car or a trip to Fiji, but it's still a reward.

A hug or a kiss, if considered appropriate, or a handshake is a way of connecting with our friends, family members, and loved ones to show we care.

Listening more attentively shows we care, and that can help us to have more effective relationships.

We meet someone at one point in time, and we often learn a lot about each other at that time. But then routine sets in, and except for the times you spend lots of hours on the phone or in person together, you may fail to find out all the details about each other that make you feel special and validated.

So instead of sharing in just the broad strokes of your life, share and receive in great detail.

Obviously, this suggestion goes somewhat against the grain of the Facebook.com era, which has hundreds of "friends" sharing in broad strokes with each other. In moderation, using Facebook.com to share about yourself and learning about what's going on with those you care about is efficient. But unless you keep the individual connections going, preferably in person, you will find your closest relationships becoming homogenized.

I am reminded of a woman I interviewed who had two so traumatic Facebook.com experiences that she had to stop visiting the site, at least for a few months till she recovered from what happened. The first experience was learning, through Facebook.com, that a close friend killed herself rather than finding out such tragic news through a phone call from one of their shared friends. The second experience was finding out, through Facebook.com once again, that her husband's daughter from a previous marriage was pregnant with her fifth child. Her father and stepmother got the news along with their stepdaughter's numerous Facebook "friends" rather than in the exclusive way that they would have preferred to find out.

If you are careful about doing anything similar—if you have really special news that one or a few people should hear first by phone or in person—then sharing the news with the rest of your universe of friends and extended family members and co-workers (if you allow work-related relationships to "friend" you) then Facebook.com might be a useful tool for strengthening those relationships that might have fallen by the wayside due to little or no communication.

Chapter 11

The Three Time Management Lessons My Father Taught Me*

Set the alarm one hour ahead so you have time for one hour of morning exercise. *[But be careful not to allow yourself to be sleep-deprived.—JY]*

—William Barkas, D.D.S.

Sometimes we learn from our parents because they are role models of what to do. I can definitely say that my father was a hard worker and he put his family first. Two admirable traits that definitely have helped me to be so successful and to have a family that is strong and committed to each other.

But there were other traits my father had that I needed to make tough decisions about—decisions that we all have to

---

* This essay is an edited and updated version of the composition published in *365 Daily Affirmations for Time Management* by Jan Yager, Ph.D., (Hannacroix Creek Books, Inc., 2011), reprinted with permission.

make when it comes to how our earliest childhood shapes us. Do I do things the same, the opposite, or some type of hybrid in-between approach that's my very own?

My father, William Barkas, D.D.S., was a dentist for 45 years. He also was a captain in the Army, serving in World War II in Africa and Europe. He was the father of three as well as a husband for 54 years to my mother when he died at the age of 80 from a brain tumor. My late father provided me with so many very powerful and enduring time management lessons, but I decided to pick the three most compelling ones to share with you. I pass along these teachings so you may also reap the benefits of these hard-won insights.

Lesson #1

Get out of the mundane day-to-day routine and spend time together, including vacations.

My father was a dedicated and hardworking dentist who worked on Saturdays and spent his one day off during the week volunteering at a clinic, so we spent little time on family trips during my formative years. Yes, my father did take my sister and me bowling and ice skating, and we went out to a movie and a fancy restaurant at least twice a year to celebrate my mother or my father's birthday. I cherished the longer leisure time together, especially those few family trips, but it was too infrequent.

I know some of you may be thinking or even saying, "Kids will never feel you give them enough time." Not true! Kids, especially older children, teens, and adult children, have a need for family or extended family time that is "just right"—not too little and not too much, so children or teens still have enough time for their school or work commitments, friends, or other meaningful relationships. I could count on just one hand the number of family vacations we took during my formative years. Those few trips loom so large in my memory bank that I do not think it is a coincidence that when my husband and I were living in Manhattan and house hunting, something inside me on a deep subliminal level called out for Connecticut, the location of one of those pivotal but infrequent family vacations when I was just three.

Yes, I gained a strong work ethic from my parents because so much of what I saw them doing when I was growing up related to work and preparing for work. That work ethic has certainly served me well in the demanding academic and professional careers I have pursued. But I learned from my father's example that a balance of work and leisure benefits everyone. I still struggle to control how much time I spend working and to have more fun in my life. When my children were little, if they had a half day at school I would plan an activity outside of the house for the afternoon. I did that because I knew that because I worked from home, I would be torn between wanting to continue working and paying attention to them. By going bowling, to a make-your-own pottery activity, or out for lunch or even ice cream, I was trying to avoid passing on to the next generation the workaholism that had plagued my earlier years. One summer, even though my husband and I were in a crunch with work, we found a way to take a ten-day trip to Italy and Paris with our sons, who were then ages nineteen and fifteen. We knew that getting the four of us together for ten days was not that easy as the boys had their own vacation and summer plans. But we all made a commitment to spending those ten days together, and it was a trip that we cherished until the next one, which we made happen before too many years went by.

Lesson #2

Sometimes you just have to stop everything and find a way to be there for those you care about.

It sounds like a cliché, but the years galloped along and suddenly I turned around and I was in my forties, married, with two children of my own, and I found out that my 80-year-old beloved father was diagnosed with a brain tumor.

The next few months were a blur as I traveled back and forth at least once a week from my Connecticut home to the hospital on the Upper East Side of Manhattan where my father was being treated. He had successfully recovered from lung cancer seven years before, so I tried to convince myself that despite the medical evidence to the contrary he was going to get over this tumor and live at least a few more years.

But I was in denial. My father was getting much worse. Within two months, his health deteriorated at such a rapid rate that one day, seemingly without warning, he lost consciousness and ceased being the father I had known, the one who ran a marathon in his sixties and took long walks with my mother well into his late seventies. The chance to have conversations with my father—about his World War II experiences, about growing up during the Depression, about his dreams or fears—was gone in an instant.

That was the second dramatic time management lesson my father taught me—don't let day-to-day obligations keep you from a priority relationship or activity. Of course, at the time there were reasons that seemed perfectly valid to explain why I could not spend more time with my father at the hospital—childcare issues, work pressures, the two-hour commute from Connecticut to the hospital in Manhattan. But once the finality of my father's situation became apparent, I realized that those reasons were pitiful excuses. I had let my day-to-day responsibilities and concerns take precedence over being there for my father even if it meant keeping a vigil at the hospital. I emerged from that somber experience determined to have a renewed commitment to the people in my life.

I feel I've been keeping that commitment in the years since my father died. Just the other day, I put aside a major project with a looming deadline to drive more than an hour away to have a reunion with an old friend I had not seen for decades. There was a time when I would have cancelled because of my work.

Lesson #3

If you fulfill your own dreams you will be more energized and joyful, you will lack regrets or "if onlys," and you will be a role model for others.

The third time management lesson my father taught me actually happened two years after his death. My mother was trying to find a document and she came upon a journal that my father had been keeping during his 64th year unbeknownst to anyone. He was documenting his thoughts during the year before his retirement. My mother gave me the diary—my father's journal of his "countdown to retirement" year as he called his journal.

As I began reading the diary, I suddenly sobbed, overwhelmed with emotion as I learned, from my father's own words, that he had hoped to become a writer after he retired.

A writer! And I never knew that about my own father! But I could have helped him with his goal. I would have enjoyed being his mentor and then, when he finished his writing, to reading his book. (I learned he had planned to write a nonfiction book about dealing with retirement.)

The sad reality—and this was the most powerful time management lesson my father taught me posthumously—was that he died, 15 years later, never having fulfilled his dream.

That was an even more powerful lesson than the first two—don't deny yourself the joy of fulfilling your dreams and goals. Fortunately, I've learned that lesson well, and just two years after my father's death my lifelong dream of having a novel published was fulfilled when a mystery I co-authored with my husband Fred, *Untimely Death*, was published. (I might have had to found my own publishing company to publish it, but that did not matter; our novel was published, and as a bonus it got excellent reviews and was even bought by a Swedish publisher that translated it into Swedish and brought us to Stockholm for an author tour of their edition.)

What dreams do you have that you are putting off?

One by one, find a way to begin fulfilling your dreams.

And even though my dad did not fulfill his dream of becoming a "self-employed author," as he put it in his diary, by keeping that diary he at least was closer to fulfilling that dream. I hope someday to make that dream come true for him by publishing his diary. In the meantime, I can reread his diary and enjoy sharing his thoughts, memories, and even remembering my father in a much more detailed way than I usually can, more than a decade after his death. For in the midst of his diary, I find a carbon copy of a letter that he wrote to me on February 24, 1980.

The contents of the letter are special and uplifting, the encouragement you'd expect a father to extend to his grown daughter. But what stays with me as I stare at the carbon copy of that letter is what I learned about my father from that letter. That he went to the trouble to make that copy of his letter to me so he could put it in his journal, so he could remember his words to me and commit those words to posterity. That's how important that letter to me was to him. He had to save a copy for himself. That says a lot to me about the man and about how he valued his communications with me.

So, as my friend Mary, who is continuing to pursue her dream of acting and directing plays, says, "Just keep on keeping on."

Chapter 12

Cultural Issues and Productivity

How we manage our time does not exist in a vacuum. Our attitudes and, hence, our productivity are influenced by such cultural issues as where we're from, what our gender is, our age, our religion. Understand what cultural issues are impacting you and your time management skills as well as those you work with, nearby and around the world.

Culture includes where we were raised as well as where we may have relocated for school or work. What age we are might even influence what time of day we go out to a restaurant, or even if we prepare our meals at home or eat out at all. Go out to dinner at 6 p.m. on a weekday night to a restaurant and you will find a very unique situation if you are doing that in a suburb of Connecticut, where parents may already be out with their children who need to get ready for school the next day; or in Madrid, Spain, where dinner might not start till 8 p.m.; or the Upper East Side of Manhattan, where the young working professionals have not even returned from their high-powered jobs yet; or in parts of Florida, some seniors will have eaten dinner an hour or two before 6 because of the lower-priced senior early bird specials.

In this chapter, we will look at time management from gender, age, and cultural perspectives so you can continue to optimize your productivity.

Gender Concerns

Are men really from Mars and are women really from Venus, as relationship expert John Gray suggested in his mega-bestselling book *Men Are from Mars and Women Are from Venus*? Or is that just a myth? And how do gender similarities and differences impact on time management?

As a sociologist, over the years I've taught classes at the college level in the role of gender, race, and class so I know that gender matters. Age, race, and culture matter too. But noting that gender matters is not the same thing as reducing time issues to stereotypical pronouncements, like girls are late or boys are better at math. Those are stereotypes, and, like all stereotypes, the exceptions are as notable as the "rules." But what we do need to consider is how gender issues impact on how we do time management and how the gender we were born to, and the roles that that gender may carve out for us, is a factor that needs to be addressed even if it is not the last word on what we plan for ourselves.

One way that gender impacts on how you do time management is that a woman, if she does want to have one or more children, needs to be concerned with what we in the West call the "biological clock" and when it's ticking louder or softer. Yes, it is biologically possible now for a woman to freeze her eggs so that, realistically, she could have one of her own eggs implanted even after her own body would have found it difficult to have a child—let's say, conservatively, at the age of 48 or 50, although typically by 35 to 40 fertility is becoming harder. But would someone want to freeze her eggs even if she or her family or loved ones are not opposed to doing that from a religious or philosophical standpoint? What would it cost to do that for a year or two, or a decade or more?

Things are changing for women in terms of career choices and options around the world, but if a woman chooses to stay home with her child or children for some time or even for prolonged time periods that will impact on her career choices. It need not impact in a negative way, however. Staying home with children, especially if a woman decides to use that as an opportunity to start a part-time or full-time business that she might not have started if she had stayed in the traditional workplace, could turn out to be the best career decision she could have made. Or it could turn out to just be a "hobby" that never becomes profitable, but it keeps her busy while she's raising her children until the time that she returns to her "real" work, whether it's at a factory, in an office, or at a university.

Men may seem to have more career choices than women around the world, but they may also be forced into making more narrow choices because of their gender; if they do choose to follow careers that are considered more "feminine," they might be subject to ridicule. A male nurse is, of course, a lot less unusual today than in bygone days; the clichés that men are doctors and women are nurses or that most librarians are female are changing.

Age Issues

And what about age? I personally am more focused and efficient as I have aged. I actually find myself speeding up in this third part of my life. What about you? Where are you in your life cycle, and how does your age influence your life decisions or how you spend your time?

Yes, there are jobs that do have age limitations, but fortunately those jobs, like police officer or firefighter or joining the FBI, are few and far between. Most jobs embrace those of all ages, and some of us even improve with time although for some, unfortunately, there are physiological changes related to age that have to be considered. The challenges, however, are not related to age as much as they're related to the physiological changes that occur because of certain diseases or disabilities that may be age-related.

I know that those changes because of age were a consideration of mine when I was choosing what to major in during college. I started out majoring in drama and even took time off from college to go to acting school. But when I returned to college, I switched my major to art. I decided that pursuing a career where I might "peak" in my 20s or 30s was less appealing than a career as an artist (which I later replaced with my decision to pursue writing as well as sociology, criminology, and business), where age was less of a factor in the staying power of that career. Ironically, I find myself thinking about going back into acting, being "shown the way" by two of my friends, Judy and Mary, who have restarted their acting careers in their senior years, undeterred by age.

Race and Ethnicity

Race is a social construct. Unfortunately, it has become one of the ways that people judge each other. There are stereotypes about how various races deal with time. Those too are social constructs. What matters is examining what your prejudices about race are, especially as it relates to time management and productivity, and rethinking why those clichés are not just untrue but slowing how you manage your time or inaccurately judging others and their efficiency.

Here is how Paula S. Rothenberg, editor of *Race, Class, and Gender in the United States: An Integrated Study,* describes race and ethnicity in the 10th edition of her textbook:

> The claim that race is a social construction challenges the once-popular belief that people are born into different races that have innate, biologically based differences in intellect, temperament, and character. The idea of ethnicity, in contract to race, focuses on the shared social/cultural experiences and heritages of various groups and divides or categorizes them according to these shared experiences and traits. The important difference here is that those who talk of race and racial identity believe that they are dividing people according to biological or genetic similarities and differences, whereas those who talk of ethnicity simply point to commonalities that are understood as social, not biological, in origin.

Whether someone is Korean or Hungarian, American or French, there are going to be ethnic similarities and differences. Even within the United States, there are wide disparities in how time is perceived, comparing the fast-paced East to the slower Southern states, for example. I was reminded of the difference in how those who live in the suburbs approach time compared to those who live in a major city, like New York, when I first went back to Manhattan for a visit and took the subway rather than driving in after living in the suburbs for a few years. I kept swiping my MetroCard to gain access to the subway, but the system kept telling me to swipe again. It seemed I wasn't swiping fast enough so the system was unable to read and register my card, no doubt the result of living in the slower-paced suburbs.

The habit of skipping lunch, or having a 30-minute lunch hunched over your desk, will be considered in a very different light if you are doing business with a company in Spain, Mexico, or another Latin America or European country.

Cultural Considerations

As noted above, the concepts of time as well as time and life management need to take cultural differences into account. For example, as I point out in my book *Grow Global*, when I asked someone at the Fiji airport about how those in Fiji approach time, the response I heard many times was, "Fiji time is no time. You can't be in a rush in Fiji."

Find out what "on time" means in the culture you are doing business with or, if you are on vacation, where you are staying. Does it mean precisely on time? Within twenty minutes of the appointed time?

When should a meeting start? Right on time, or within ten or twenty minutes or longer? I remember an executive from a major New York financial services company telling me that his company would lock the door at the exact time a meeting was supposed to commence; you could not enter after that time no matter how legitimate your reason for being late.

Would you find the same response in Abu Dhabi? Mumbai? Barcelona? Los Angeles? Nashville? You will want to find out the answer to that question if you want to know how they manage their time in each of those places if you are doing business with that culture.

There are, however, time concerns that are quite universal for those of us who are in business. Here is the response I received from a young businessman in Mumbai, Veerendra Nayak, in answer to my query about productivity concerns:

> Time management was one of my biggest concerns even when I was a student. I chose to become an entrepreneur back in year 2008 when I was only 22. For the first 12–18 months, I struggled like crazy to get started. I faced a variety of problems every step on the way, but I fought hard and never gave up. Now I'm successfully running a low investment, high profit Internet business model for the past 2–3 years. I had a variety of bad habits, like not being serious about work and life, procrastinating things, not listing and organizing events, taking things for granted, and so on. I had to put in extra efforts to become punctual and efficient in the early stage of my entrepreneurship or succeeding further would have been nearly impossible. It did take me a while, but I succeeded with the help of books on business and management and of course my willingness to change.

Chapter 13

Eleven Top Time Management Concepts for Greater Productivity

> Remember that time is money.
> —BENJAMIN FRANKLIN

Out of all the time management and productivity training I've done, here are my eleven favorite concepts that should help you to be more productive. These concepts were discussed in greater detail throughout this book. Refer back to those sections if you want more examples or anecdotes. This is a summary that will hopefully empower you as you go forward taking better control of how you spend each and every minute of each and every day of your precious life:

1. Overcome procrastination so you can do your priorities.

Understand, and deal with, procrastination so you don't waste your valuable time ruminating over things you *should* be doing.

2. See a deadline as a line that gives you life and power rather than seeing a deadline as something that is negative.

Make sure your deadlines are realistic. A realistic deadline will motivate you. A deadline that is too soon or unrealistic may discourage you or even "shut you down."

If you have agreed to a deadline that won't work, as soon as you realize the situation, explain why and, if possible, negotiate for a new time frame. Don't wait till the last minute so you'll be seen as someone who's disorganized and unproductive. If the deadline cannot be changed, see what time-saving strategies you can implement, such as delegating to others—staff members or outsourcing to freelancers—or to technology or even revising the goal.

3. RRA: Respond Right Away.

Don't just let requests sit there, ignored "till I get the time to respond" because you're always going to be pressed for time. Ignored requests from those who matter can lead to animosity and projects that get off track or even relationships that end. Even just telling someone, "I'll get back to you," is better than ignoring someone.

If you're not the right person to handle an inquiry, delegate that inquiry to someone else, even if it's to the technology of an "auto-responder," rather than ignoring it. Being polite is a sign of business protocol as well as heightened efficiency.

I think back on the CEOs I've personally and professionally known and been impressed by and communicated with, and they were always responsive—either personally or they had their executive assistants communicate. At a lower level than that, an "auto-responder" can at least report something like, "Closed for the holidays. Please write back in 10 days."

4. WOO: *Window of Opportunity*

One of the greatest benefits of improved efficiency to get done what you have to do is that it frees up your time to seize those opportunities that do come along. You're not behind the eight ball, so to speak, so you have to put off responding to a wonderful new opportunity that could make all the difference in your business or career success.

Learn how to recognize those WOOs and you are more likely to see amazing positive improvements in how much, and what, you are accomplishing.

What *window of opportunity* (WOO) experiences are you opening yourself up to, whether it's through e-mail and social media sites, like LinkedIn.com or Twitter.com, or through face-to-face meetings at conferences or introductions that you facilitate through those you work with, for, or even your friends and family? Are you promptly and appropriately following up on those introductions or meetings?

5. *Use e-mail; don't let it misuse you.*

Use e-mail and the Internet in the service of your job and not as a time waster or as a distraction. Nina Roesner, the productive homeschool mom you first heard about in Chapter 9, "Using the P.I.E.," shares her e-mail tip: "I don't open e-mail until 2 p.m. Okay, maybe after lunch. But if it is all that important, they would have called. In looking at e-mail later in the day, I am able to manage my time instead of reacting to other people's agendas."

What's important is that that tip works for Nina. Consider that tip. Would it work for you? For me, I must look at e-mail first thing in the morning because so much of what I do is international, so key e-mails may arrive in the morning that were sent from Asia or Europe while I was still asleep. But I've learned *not* to respond to an e-mail unless it's *my priority*. I might glance over the e-mails I've received during the night, but I only respond when it's convenient for me. But if I'm really "in the zone" on a project and under deadline pressure, I might use Nina Roesner's tactic of not looking at e-mails till later in the day. Or I might not even look at the e-mails I've received till after I've finished my priority task, whatever time that turns out to be.

6. Find out how others prefer to be contacted and use that way of communicating for a better likelihood of more effective interaction and outcome.

If someone lets you know that he or she hates phone calls, respect that. If e-mail is his or her preference, follow that lead— although of course if you continually use the same method of communicating and it does not get a response, at least check that the individual was receiving your communications or try another way, explaining that's why you're doing it. For example, send a fax to find out if your e-mail was received or leave a voicemail pointing out that you sent several e-mails. Sometimes e-mails may get lost in cyberspace.

7. Review, review, review.

Make sure whatever you complete and turn in, whether it's a project or a proposal, has been checked and rechecked. If possible, have someone else proofread your work because it's easy for typos or misspellings to slip in when you're rereading your own work.

8. We're defined as much by what we say "no" to as by what we say "yes" to, so if this is a challenge for you,

learn how to say "no" politely and tactfully without feeling guilty about it.

None of us can do everything. We have to choose the people we hang out with and the projects we will take on. If a project is not right for you, it's okay to say "no," unless of course it's the boss asking you to do it and you have to say "yes" or risk falling out of favor or even losing your job. If you are overcommitted for volunteer work in your community, let others know that. Don't be afraid to say "no."

There's a cliché that if you want to get something done, ask the busiest person to do it. That may be true, but it's also unfair, especially if you're that busy one who's always getting asked. That may be why there are those who are reluctant to volunteer in the first place. They're afraid it will take over their life. But being able to feel comfortable with what you say "yes" or "no" to will help you to broaden your options and empower you in how you spend your time.

9. OTD: Out the Door

You know if you're making progress because you're getting projects OTD (out the door). You're not just spinning your wheels without seeing results. OTD, by the way, means you are meeting your goals. It need not always be something that is "physically" going out the door.

It doesn't have to take over your life. It goes back to what we looked at in Chapter 4, "Self-management and Self-confidence." You are in control. You can do this, but say "no" to that and the other thing. You can even say "maybe" but be very careful with those maybes. Maybes can sometimes be a good tactic. It gives you time to ponder and think and consider or reconsider. Or it can slow you down and be a delaying tactic with the consequence of inaction. For example, I knew an acquisitions editor at a publishing company who, years ago, was so ambivalent about saying "yes" to projects that he was saying "maybe" to everyone and not signing up any new books. After a year or so of that, his boss had to let him go because he wasn't "growing his list." Yes, he avoided making mistakes by not signing up any new book that might turn out to be a disappointment, but he also wasn't generating new projects that had the potential to be successful.

10. Look outside your own frame of reference to other professions or fields for inspiration and insights, as well as to other cultures.

Too many of us get stuck in the rut of looking to our own fields. For example, whether that's publishing companies for writers and authors, advertising companies for those in advertising, sociology if you're a sociologist, financial services if you're in the finance field, or other travel agencies if you're in the travel business and so forth. Instead, stretch yourself and see where it takes you. If you're a sociologist, consider partnering with a neurologist and see where that might lead you both. If you're a psychologist, consider attending the annual conference for doctors, nurses, and trainers in sports medicine to see what you might learn and where that might lead you.

You could also look to other cultures for insights into dissimilar ways of doing things, whether it's from someone within your own country or another country nearby or thousands of miles away. For example, psychologist Dr. Wayne Dyer read through the sayings of Lao Tse, which he put together in a book entitled *Change Your Thought, Change Your Life.*

11. D-O I-T N-O-W

If you have a great idea, do something about it immediately because the longer you dwell on it and fail to act on it, the greater the chances it will get out there in the universe and someone else will do it before you. We're in a world where if you blink, you're too late. The same is true with those projects you know you have to do, for your boss or for yourself. That website that needs to be redesigned or even getting a website up in the first place. That blog you need to commit to writing every day. You know what that priority task is so D-O I-T N-O-W.

In *Creative Time Management for the New Millennium* (Hannacroix Creek Books, 1999, reprinted with permission), D-O I-T N-O-W stood for the following:

- **D** = **D**ivide and conquer what you have to do. Break big tasks into little tasks and give each part of that task a realistic deadline.

- **O** = **O**rganize your materials, how you will do it.

- **I** = **I**gnore interruptions that are annoying distractions.

- **T** = **T**ake the time to learn how to do things yourself.

- **N** = **N**ow, not tomorrow. Don't procrastinate.

- **O** = **O**pportunity is knocking. Take advantage of opportunities.

- **W** = **W**atch out for time globbers. Keep track of, and in control of, how much time you spend on the Internet, reading and sending e-mails, watching TV, or talking on the phone.

Now let's consider how you are going to move forward in your time management skills and your life management goal as we turn to the last chapter in this book.

Chapter 14

Going Forward As You Put More Time on Your Side

Returning to the theme of this book—that time management is life management—reapply the skills YOU have learned, or had reinforced, in this book as you go through your life, as you enter atypical phases and stages. What are your priorities now? How have things changed for you in terms of your physical, mental, emotional, and motor skills and capabilities that you need to address in your everyday life?

In this last chapter, as you look ahead, let's take some time to apply to your life some of the key concepts you've acquired in this book.

Learn This Acronym: ACHIEVE

Here is an acronym that will help you with how you do your own time management. Each letter stands for a separate word and concept, and because we are all concerned with this topic—how we can achieve—you are more likely to remember the acronym and each of the words.

A = Aim

Aim high, but most important—aim. Aiming is the same thing as setting a goal. Your goal is what you are aiming to accomplish or achieve.

C = Clarify

Make sure you are clear about what you need to do, and keep your workspace and your mind clear. Organize your space. Don't try to operate in a mess, or if you have a mess, when you get a break in your work clean it up.

A messy desk is not a sign of genius. It's a sign of a messy desk.

H = Hone in on what is important to do.

This is another way of saying *prioritize*.

Do what you have to do and say "no" or "not now" to everything and everyone else.

I = Innovate

We all have a little of the Steve Jobs visionary "gene" or capability in us if we just give ourselves a chance. By getting done what you have to do, you free up time to let your imagination soar. Some of your innovations may be silly or inconsequential. But *let yourself innovate*. It's good practice as you fail toward success. I remember one of my first innovations was a pink satin typewriter cover that I handmade and sent the picture of that creation to *Seventeen* magazine. I explained in the essay that accompanied my innovation that it would enable other young girls—I was around 12 or 13 at the time—to put a lovely cover over their typewriters so it wouldn't look so ugly sitting in the corner of their room. I didn't realize back then that most girls my age didn't have a typewriter in their room!

E = Educate

Keep learning, whether it's at school or on your own. Using your brain will not just help keep your brain working longer and better, but you will be learning about new innovations in how to save time that are being created and written about. Yes, there is what is called an information overload, but there is also valuable and useful knowledge being shared each and every day. Never stop reading or learning and sharing what you learn with others.

V = Vision

Think of that time in your life when you were most success-ful, most innovative, most creative. Think to when you were closest to doing what you love and achieving what you want to achieve. What were you doing then that you're not doing now? How can you start making those visions happen again, whatever your age or current occupation? As my father used to say, "While there's life, there's hope," so there is hope for you. You can make your dreams come true for the first time or, if you were fortunate enough to have that happen before, again and again.

E = Evaluate

We all have to keep evaluating what we are doing. Is it working now even if it worked yesterday, last week, or twenty years ago? But does it work *now*? If not, what do I have to do to make it work?

If you put into practice ACHIEVE, you will be much more likely to look back at the end of the year that you are currently living with personal and professional successes. Remember that you are in control of your time and your life. You can make each day as productive as you decide it will be. You are not a puppet on anyone else's strings.

Are You a 50 Percent or a 100 Percent Person?

In a previous part of this book, we looked at how to connect with the movers and shakers in your business. That's an ongoing consideration because who those movers and shakers are may change as your role at work changes or even as the type of work you do shifts. But you also want to be putting the time into yourself and your career so that if becoming one of those movers and shakers is one of your goals, you are working harder to achieve that goal. I know that for me, the relationship between how many books I'm selling is usually directly proportionate to the amount of time and energy I put into that part of the writing process. I had to learn the hard way that being an author is 50 percent writing a book and 50 percent selling it. Too many authors fail to have the wider audience that they might have because they are doing only 50 percent of their job. (And the 50 percent that goes into selling might mean going on TV and radio, giving speeches or workshops, or making a book trailer that goes viral on YouTube.com. There's no one way to make that goal happen, but it still needs to be a goal and to be part of one's time.)

This concept does not apply to just book authors, of course! It applies to all of us. For example, I was giving a workshop on time management to a group of fifty men and women who worked for or ran businesses of various sizes. I asked everyone to take a few moments to write down a brief description of what they were initially hired to do. I then asked them, based on what they now know about their job, what they have learned are the key tasks they should be doing, how they are judged as being successful performers on their job, and to reorder those tasks with the number one task they should be doing as the first task.

Then I asked them to write down the percentage of their day that they were spending on that task.

I then asked for volunteers to share the results of that exercise.

A woman raised her hand and she said that the number one task that she should be doing on her job was making *sales*.

"So how much of your day do you spend each day on selling?" I asked.

I was anticipating her answer would be 10 percent or 25 percent or maybe even 50 percent. But instead she said, "Zero."

There was a collective gasp in the room, but practically everyone could relate to what she said.

I asked her to share what she was doing with her time at work and she explained that her day had become a blur of responding to the requests of others as well as doing lots of low-priority activities that just seemed to consume her day so that she could not point to a specific accomplishment each day. But she assured me and the rest of the workshop attendees that she was very busy.

Sound familiar? Could that be you? Or, if it's not you now, have there been times that you fell into a similar situation? You were spending lots of time getting things done, but it wasn't the activities that were moving you ahead the way you wanted to be propelled either professionally or personally.

Take a long, hard look at your own job or career. What is the part of what you do each day or week that comes most easily to you—your 50 percent where you're spending half or even more of your day? Now consider what is that other 50 percent, the half that perhaps you do not like to do or you never seem to get around to doing, but you know that is the half that you know will catapult your career to the top (or even the 20 percent if you apply Pareto's 80/20 law to this equation—20 percent of your efforts will get you 80 percent of your results)?

Now make a commitment to make putting the time into that 50 percent a priority for you. Make a decision that today, and going forward, you will be a 100 percent person, making the most of each and every day so you see the short- and long-term results that will turn this day and the next year into your most productive ever.

Measuring Improvements in Your Time Management

As part of your time management self-improvement program, I want you to ask yourself how you will measure that *you* have improved your time management skills. What are the quantitative or qualitative ways that you will know you are better off after reading this book, and considering what you have learned, than you were before? Read over the possibilities below, and if your own measure for better time management mastery is missing, add it to the list:

- I am happier.

- I feel more in control.

- I am generating more revenue. I am making more money.

- I have a clearer focus about what's important to me.

- I am spending more time on my priority projects.

- I figured out what my 100 percent job requirements are to be successful, and I'm working on all 100 percent, not 50 percent.

- I identified and I'm working on overcoming the time wasters that have been holding me back.

- I'm spending more time with my family.

- I'm getting to hang out more with my friends.

- I read a novel for fun for the first time in years.

- My spouse and I planned a vacation and we made a promise to each other not to cancel at the last minute this time.

- I'm on time more regularly.

- I've been meeting or beating deadlines.

- I feel an inner calm.

- I spend at least 30 minutes to an hour each day thinking.

- I've been getting praised lately for getting more done.

- Instead of excusing any of my shortcomings, I'm working on improving.

- I welcome and learn from feedback.
- I'm thinking ahead more.
- I am setting short-term and long-term goals for myself and for my job.
- I feel that my life is in balance.

Yes, there are as many ways to measure that you're more effectively managing your time as there are readers. We are all unique, and what you or I might want at this point in our lives is probably very different, but it can also change as we age or our children grow up or our interests shift. Or perhaps the act of mastery of a task makes you want to shift to another job or even a completely different career where you will have fresh challenges. Bravo!

\ Making Time for Relationships

Yes, we have to make time for our work, for all the requirements of our jobs, but we also need to make time for our relationships—with our spouse or romantic partner; with our children, whatever their ages, whether two, twenty, or fifty; with our extended family; with our friends; with our neighbors; but we also have to make time for a relationship with ourselves. Whether that means taking a class that you've put off taking, going to the gym, taking a long walk, or going on a trip, with someone or alone, even if it's to the movies or to a new restaurant—giving yourself quality time needs to be a priority.

Having a Commitment to Lifelong Learning

Your commitment to lifelong learning might mean that you make sure you put in the time to keep up in your field or that you embrace new hobbies and interests that expand your horizon. That you explore through live theater as well as cinema, TV, or Internet programming—a growing way to get new content—so you expand your horizons and you keep learning. Also you visit websites for information, although you always have to be concerned about the credibility and reliability of the information that you're accessing.

Becoming More Self-Directed

As life expectancy improves around the world so that the post-retirement years may be as long or even longer than the working years, becoming more self-directed is a skill that will take you far. You will not waste the time in your retirement because you are bored, lacking the structure and direction that a typical eight to six or nine to five job offers you. In the same way, the at-home parent who has devoted herself to her children needs to have a new direction once her children leave the nest and are "launched," so that she can now devote herself to new activities, whether that will be going back to work, volunteering in her community, or even going back to school.

Are there any changes in your life that you need to be focusing on that will impact on the work you do or even where you live? Perhaps you have a child with disabilities who requires you and your family to relocate so he can attend a special school? Or maybe the company you were working for has offered you a big promotion if you're willing to move to another part of the country, far away from your familiar surroundings? Maybe your knees are giving you problems, so you want to move to a new apartment or home on one level, if walking has become a challenge? Maybe try getting closer to an urban situation if the quiet and necessity of driving in the suburbs or country will no longer work for you. Or, by contrast, you find that you prefer the quiet even after decades living and working in the midst of a bustling city.

After my grandfather died and my grandmother was left alone with two grown children and a sixteen-year-old who was close to maturity, she went to work as a seamstress. For more than twenty-five years, until she remarried, work was a big part of her life. After she retired, and after her second marriage ended, my grandmother found herself in one of the earliest assisted living residences with an assigned roommate whom she did not like and without any joy in her typical day. She tried going to the arts and crafts activities that were offered, but she just never felt at home in that residence; for that last decade or more of her life, she seemed sad whenever I visited her.

I was a single career woman, self-employed, and although I would have occasional periods of full-time employment as an academic or as a foreign rights consultant, most of my adult years I have been on my own, creating my own schedule. Of course, during the years I was raising our two sons, whether I was working or not I had to be concerned with our sons' school schedules as well as my husband's employer's schedule.

I remember telling my grandmother, who during one visit told me she was worried about me because I was self-employed, that being self-employed was actually the best training I knew of for those later years of retirement. I was very familiar with filling up my time in a productive way.

The Best Laid Plans of Mice and Men

That is one of my favorite phrases and concepts to help me get through the challenges that occur that are out of my control. Think of all the times you had everything under control. You were working at an optimum pace. You had your own time wasters "in check" so you were as efficient as you had ever been. And then, voila, something happens that you could not have planned for. A family member gets sick or passes away suddenly. Your boss asks you to shift gears and put aside whatever you're doing and work on a different project. Your child asks you if you could help out with something that's going to take hours of your time, hours you had already planned for something else, but you decide it's best to be there for your child instead.

When these changes happen, it's best to just "go with the flow" and to grant yourself the opportunity to do what you now have to do. You will get back on track. You may actually find that you do better than you would have done if you had never had this detour. Maybe it's because of what you learn from the detour. Maybe it's because you forge a stronger relationship with your child, and that gives you the emotional and psychological strength to feel better about yourself and work more effectively than ever before. Maybe because you really needed a break but you wouldn't have voluntarily given yourself one, but these unforeseen circumstances are forcing you to slow down so you can speed up.

Time Choices

After all, the time we have on earth is so short in the scheme of things. There is not one second to waste. That, in a nutshell, is how you *do* time management. You use the skills in this quirky pseudo-discipline known as time management to get more done faster, and most of all you improve your ability to make the tough judgment calls about what you should be doing in the first place. That includes everything from the people you should be hanging out with to the projects you should be working on to the books you should be reading to the events you should be participating in.

Let's not go backward to the days when people were working sixteen hour days, six or even seven days a week. We've made positive gains in better work conditions, and we should not let that wonderful innovation and invention the cell phone and the smartphone turn us into work machines with the ability to have 24/7 e-mail communications and phone calls. You can shut your phone off. You are in control. You don't have to throw your phone into the lake so you stop yourself from answering it or sending a text message. It's great that the technology is there, but use the technology in the service of your time and life, not with it making you its slave.

I have also noticed that the interest in time management can ebb and flow with the economy. When people have more disposable income so that they are able to hire more assistants to do the work that they prefer to avoid doing, there is less interest in time management than when it becomes more necessary to do everything yourself. It is then that there is a tendency to look to time management for the "answers"—how can you do more in less time and with fewer resources?

Time management skills and concerns should not depend on whether or not the economy is doing well or upon your own personal financial situation. Just because you can afford to hire an executive assistant to answer your phone for you does not mean it will be the best way to handle business communications for you. You just might be missing out on many potential business opportunities; in your case, have two or three distinctive phone numbers with your assistant handling just one number, which is the "public" number, while you always answer the second "private" number because that number is only given out to very important people—the movers and shakers who want to talk to you and no one else. That might be a better solution for you.

I also invite you to reread this book as your life changes because you will react to the concepts and suggestions differently based on your circumstances. And that's okay. In fact, that's great. We all need to be flexible as we reapply basic concepts to our situation as those relationships or jobs evolve.

Thank you for going on this productivity journey with me. I hope I have been a worthwhile guru. Please let me know by e-mail how this little book has helped you with your productivity challenges. You can write to me via e-mail at jyager@aol.com. And keep me in mind if you, your company, or your association want me to offer a presentation, workshop, seminar, or individual or group coaching sessions on time management.

One more thought: *priority management* seems to be the preferred term these days for what we've been calling *time management*. I really like that alternative phrase and concept! It emphasizes one of the cornerstones of my own productivity philosophy and teachings as well as the key theme to *Put More Time on Your Side:* know what your priorities are, and accomplish each one, whether in your business or personal life, and your time will be well spent!

Selected Bibliography
Including Works Cited

Allen, David. *Getting Things Done*. New York: Penguin, 2001.

Aubrey, Allison. "Move Around on Long Flights to Prevent Blood Clots." Heard on NPR "Morning Edition." Posted at http://www.npr.org/templates/story/story.php?storyId=12593776.

Barkas, J.L. (a.k.a. Jan Yager) *Creative Time Management*. Englewood Cliffs, NJ: Prentice-Hall, Inc., 1984.

Blanchard, Ken, and Spencer Johnson. *The One-Minute Manager*. New York: William Morrow, 1982.

Blanke, Gail. *Throw Fifty Things Out*. New York: Grand Central Publishing, 2010.

Canfield, Jack, et. al., *The Power of Focus*. HCI, 2000.

Catalyst Inc. "Work-Life Effectiveness in Asia: One Size Doesn't Fit All." Press release dated May 16, 2012, received via e-mail on 5/16/2012.

Christensen, Clayton M. "How Will You Measure Your Life?" Reprinted in *On Managing Yourself*. (*HBR's 10 Must Reads*.) Boston, Massachusetts: Harvard Business Review Press, 2010, pages 1–32. (Originally published in June 1999.)

Coutu, Diane L. "How Resilience Works." Reprinted in *On Managing Yourself.* (*HBR's 10 Must Reads.*) Boston, Massachusetts: Harvard Business Review Press, 2010, pages 47–60. (Originally published May 2002.)

Covey, Stephen R. *The 7 Habits of Highly Effective People.* New York: Simon & Schuster, Inc., 1989.

"Famous Business Partnerships." Posted at http://images. businessweek.com/ss/08/11/1121_famous_partnerships/6.htm.

Duhigg, Charles. *The Power of Habit.* New York: Random House, 2012.

Frankl, Viktor E. *Man's Search for Meaning.* Foreword by Harold S. Kushner. Boston: Beacon Press, 2006. (Originally published 1959.)

Franklin, Benjamin. *Poor Richard's Almanac.* Reprinted as an e-book by Seven Treasures Publications. (Originally published annually between 1732 and 1758.)

Friedman, Stewart D. "Be a Better Leader, Have a Richer Life." Reprinted in *On Managing Yourself.* (*HBR's 10 Must Reads.*) Boston, Massachusetts: Harvard Business Review Press, 2010, pages 97–114. (Originally published in April 2008.)

Gandel, Stephen. "The 25 Most Influential Business Management Books." Time.com, August 9, 2011, Posted at http://www.time.com/time/specials/packages/article/0,28804,2086680_2086683_2087685,00.html (Retrieved 1/2/2013.)

Ghoshal, Sumantra and Heike Bruch. "Reclaim Your Job." Reprinted in *On Managing Yourself.* (*HBR's 10 Must Reads.*) Boston, Massachusetts: Harvard Business Review Press, 2010, pages 115–126. (Originally published in March 2004.)

Goffman, Erving. *The Presentation of Self in Everyday Life.* New York: Penguin, 1990. (Originally published in 1956.)

Goleman, Daniel, Richard Boyatzis, and Annie McKee. "Primal Leadership: The Hidden Driver of Great Performance." Reprinted in *On Managing Yourself.* (*HBR's 10 Must Reads.*) Boston, Massachusetts: Harvard Business Review Press, 2010, pages 169-188. (Originally published in December 2001.)

John Gray. Men Are from Mars and Women Are from Venus. New York: HarperCollins, 1993.

Hall, Edward T. The Dance of Life: The Other Dimension of Time. New York: Anchor, 1984.

Hallowell, Edward M. "Overloaded Circuits." Reprinted in *On Managing Yourself.* (*HBR's 10 Must Reads.*) Boston, Massachusetts: Harvard Business Review Press, 2010, pages 79–95. (Originally published in January 2005.)

Harvard School of Public Health. "The Obesity Prevention Source." Posted at http://www.hsph.harvard.edu/obesity-prevention -source/obesity-consequences/health-effects/index.html.

Huber, Laura. *The Life Planner.* Telemachus Press, Florida, 2011.

Hurwitz, Cipora. *Forbidden Strawberries.* Translated from the Hebrew. Westchester, NY: Multieducator, 2010.

Ilibagiza, Immaculee with Steve Erwin. *Left to Tell: Discovering God Amidst the Rwadan Holocaust.* CA: Hay House, 2007.

Kaplan, Robert S. "What to Ask the Person in the Mirror." Reprinted in *On Managing Yourself.* (*HBR's 10 Must Reads.*) Boston, Massachusetts: Harvard Business Review Press, 2010, pages 147–167. (Originally published in January 2007.)

Keller, Greg and Jay Papasan. *The One Thing.* Bard Press, 2013.

Konigsberg, Eric. "A U.S. Writer's Easy-going Perfectionism." *International Herald Tribune,* October 16, 2009, page 10.

Lakein, Alan. How to Get Control of Your Time and Your Life. New York: Signet, 1989.

Mackenzie, Alex with Pat Nickerson. *The Time Trap.* Revised edition. New York: AMACOM, 2009.

McKeown, Greg. *Essentialism.* New York: Crown Business, 2014.

Morgenstern, Julie. *Never Check E-mail in the Morning.* New York: Simon & Schuster, Inc., Fireside Books, 2005.

_____. *Time Management from the Inside Out.* 2nd edition. New York: Holt, 2004.

Murali, Rekha. "Time management for new mothers." Posted on December 26, 2012 at http://www.thehindu.com/todays-paper/tp-features/tp-opportunities/time-management-for-new-mothers/article4239936.ece.

Nayak, Veerendra. "The 7 Key Secrets of Internet Business Success" (available at www.7KeySecrets.com).

"New high speed train passes central China." Posted at http://english.cntv.cn/program/newsupdate/20121226/105673.shtml.

Oncken, William, Jr. and Donald L. Wass. "Management Time: Who's Got the Monkey?" Reprinted in *On Managing Yourself.* (*HBR's 10 Must Reads.*) Boston, Massachusetts: Harvard Business Review Press, 2010, pages 33–45. (Originally published in November 1999.)

Patchett, Ann. "The Bookstore Strikes Back." Posted at http://www.theatlantic.com/magazine/archive/2012/12/the-bookstore-strikes-back/309164.

Pozen, Robert C. *Extreme Productivity.* New York: HarperCollins Publishers, Inc., 2012.

Quinn, Robert E. "Moments of Greatness: Entering the Fundamental State of Leadership." Reprinted in *On Managing Yourself.* (*HBR's 10 Must Reads.*) Boston, Massachusetts: Harvard Business Review Press, 2010, pages 127–145. (Originally published in July 2005.)

Robbins, Tony. *Awaken the Giant Within.* New York: Free Press, 2007.

Rothenberg, Paula S., editor, with Soniya Munshi. *Race, Class, and Gender in the United States: An Integrated Study.* Tenth edition. New York: Worth Publishers, Macmillan Learning, 2016.

Schwartz, Tony and Catherine McCarthy. "Manage Your Energy, Not Your Time." Reprinted in *On Managing Yourself.* (*HBR's 10 Must Reads.*) Boston, Massachusetts: Harvard Business Review Press, 2010, pages 61–78. (Originally published in October 2007.)

Sexton, Timothy. "A History of the Weekend." Posted at http://voices.yahoo.com/a-history-weekend-773557.html?cat=9.

Sopher, Philip. "Where the Five-Day Workweek Came From." *The Atlantic*, August 21, 2014. Posted at http://www.theatlantic.com/business/archive/2014/08/where-the-five-day-workweek-came-from/378870.

Taylor, Frederick Winslow. *The Principles of Scientific Management.* Originally published in 1911. This edition published by Digireads.com Publishing in 2011.

Tierney, John. "Be It Resolved." *Sunday Review, New York Times,* January 8, 2012, pages 1, 6.

Wikipedia.com. "Eight-hour day." Posted at http://en.wikipedia.org/wiki/Eight-hour_day.

Yager, Jan. *125 Ways to Meet the Love of Your Life.* Second Edition. Stamford, CT: Hannacroix Creek Books, 2016.

_____. *365 Daily Affirmations for Time Management.* Stamford, CT: Hannacroix Creek Books, 2011.

_____. *Creative Time Management.* See Barkas, J.L.

_____. *Creative Time Management for the New Millennium.* Stamford, CT: Hannacroix Creek Books, Inc., 1999.

_____. *Grow Global.* Stamford, CT: Hannacroix Creek Books, 2011.

_____. *Productive Relationships.* Stamford, CT: Hannacroix Creek Books, 2011.

_____. *Fast Track Guide to Speaking in Public.* Stamford, CT: Hannacroix Creek Books, 2013.

_____. *When Friendship Hurts.* New York: Simon and Schuster, Touchstone, 2002.

_____. *Who's That Sitting at My Desk?* Stamford, CT: Hannacroix Creek Books, 2004.

_____. *Work Less, Do More.* 3rd edition. New York: Hannacroix Creek Books, 2017. (1st edition published in 2008 by Sterling Publishing, New York.)

Zerubavel, Eviatar. *Hidden Rhythms: Schedules and Calendars in Social Life.* Chicago: University of Chicago Press, 1981.

Zwilling, Marty. "Ten Productivity Mantras for Entrepreneurs." Published at Forbes.com on July 31, 2012. Posted at http:// www.forbes.com/sites/martinzwilling/2012/07/31/10-personal -productivity-mantras-for-entrepreneurs.

Resources

Inclusion in this list does not imply an endorsement nor does omission indicate anything negative about products or websites that are missing. This listing is for information purposes only. Furthermore, websites may change or even disappear from the Internet. Evaluate each and every listing on your own.

Productivity Apps/Websites

Evernote

https://evernote.com: Free app for writing everything down and keeping track of your goals.

Paper

http://www.fiftythree.com: Developed by FiftyThree, Inc. Available through iTunes, this app enables you to make lists, draw, and do related tasks.

OneNote

https://www.onenote.com: Developed by Microsoft and available for free to put notes and to-do lists on your computer, phone, or tablet.

Dropbox

www.dropbox.com: Convenient way to store key documents that you can access from anywhere. Has a free version but there is a cap on how much storage you can get. After that, there are various payment plans for more storage space.

Goal-setting Programs

https://www.stickk.com: Based on the concept of a Commitment Contract, this program was co-founded by Yale University professors including Economic Professor Dean Karlan. Other founders are Jordan Goldberg and Ian Ayres. Although the examples at the site are based on quite hefty financial incentives, you could certainly use the concept with less costly rewards.

http://weekplan.net: Inspired by Covey's *The 7 Habits of Highly Effective People* and Allen's *Getting Things Done,* developed by Aymeric Gaurat-Apelli. Has a free plan and plans with more features for a fee.

http://lifetick.com: Fee-based service ($39/month) developed by an Australian company in 2008, Meridian 86, that is also based on the SMART criteria for goal-setting.

http://goalbot.org: This goal-setting program has a three-step approach:

1. Learn about how to achieve your goals.

2. Create a detailed action plan for achieving them.

3. Connect with others who might help you to accomplish your goal.

Miscellaneous Websites

https://www.lumosity.com: Site that offers building concentration activities.

www.LinkedIn.com: Storing your business connections through this global database with more than 450 million users. Ideally you will already have some sort of connection to those you are linked to, but in reality a lot of businesspeople connect to those who are unknown to them but with whom they would like to develop a connection.

www.Timeanddate.com: Free cite that enables you to figure out what time it is anywhere in the world at that moment in case you want to make a phone call to someone or send a text message and you would prefer that it not arrive in the middle of the night!

www.xe.com: Free and quick way to find out how much a currency is worth in another currency. Just put the amount of money you want to convert in the current currency, and then put in the currency you want to convert to, click on the conversion "button," and you'll have your answer instantly.

www.timeman.com: The website for Peter Turla, who conducts time management training.

www.Twitter.com: This free site offers you a chance to grow your platform or build a brand for yourself, your product, or your company. You can also try to connect to movers and shakers by following and commenting on their tweets.

www.drjanyager.com: My website where you'll find a self-quiz to see if your time management skills could need improvement as well as excerpts of articles I've written on time management and my original blog that often deals with time management topics.

http://www.drjanyager.com/blog

Keeping a Daily Time Log

To gain control of your time and to increase your productivity, learn how your time is being spent. Use this daily log so you see where you are spending your time, what you are doing, for how long, and where you are wasting it. Track at least one workday, including your evening, and one weekend day and evening and review what you learn about yourself.

You may wish to start your daily log with the time you wake up and end it with the time you go to sleep. If you wish to keep track of more than one day of work and one day of leisure, make copies of these logs before you fill each one in so you have extra blank logs available to you. If you prefer, you may of course also track how you are spending your time in your appointment book, on your smartphone, or use one of the productivity apps that enable you to track that way.

Daily Log #1 (For a Work Day)

Day _____

Date _____

Time Activity

_____ *Wake up*

_____

_____

_____

_____

_____

_____

_____

_____

_____

_____

_____

_____

_____

_____

_____

_____

_____

_____

_____

_____

_____

Daily Log #2 (For a Leisure Day)

Day _____

Date _____

Time Activity

_____ *Wake up*

_____

_____

_____

_____

_____

_____

_____

_____

_____

_____

_____

_____

_____

_____

_____

_____

_____

_____

_____

_____

_____

Put more TIME on your side

_____

_____

_____

_____

_____

_____

_____

_____

_____

_____

_____

_____

_____

_____

_____

_____

_____

_____

_____

_____

_____

_____

_____

_____

_____

_____

_____

ACTION! Strategy Worksheet*

Project or Task: _____

A (Assess):

_____
_____
_____
_____
_____
_____
_____
_____
_____
_____
_____
_____
_____
_____
_____
_____
_____

C (Control):

_____
_____
_____
_____
_____
_____

_____

_____

_____

_____

_____

_____

_____

_____

_____

_____

T (Target):

_____

_____

_____

_____

_____

_____

_____

_____

_____

_____

_____

_____

_____

_____

I (Innovate):

O (Organize):

_____

_____

_____

_____

_____

_____

N (Now!):

_____

_____

_____

_____

_____

_____

_____

_____

_____

_____

_____

_____

_____

_____

*Excerpted and edited from *Work Less, Do More* by Jan Yager, Ph.D. (Hannacroix Creek Books, Inc.)

What Is Your P-I-E for Today?

P = PRIORITIZE

I = INITIATE

E = EVALUATE

Gain control of your time and accomplish more by being clear on how you will spend (or spend) each hour and each day. Four sample P-I-Es follow. Review your P-I-Es by applying what P-I-E stands for: Prioritize, Initiate, and Evaluate.

Use any of these P-I-Es to plan (or monitor) each hour, day, week, or even your year for greater productivity.

P-I-E #1

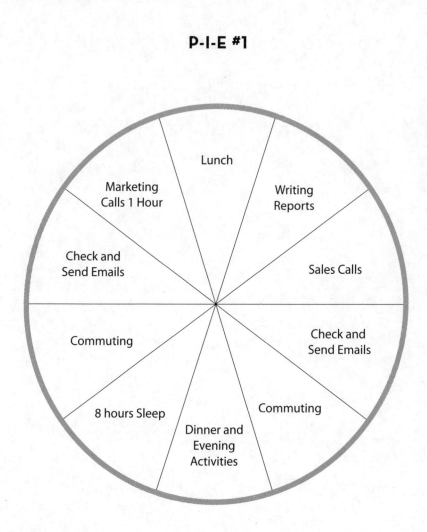

P-I-E #2

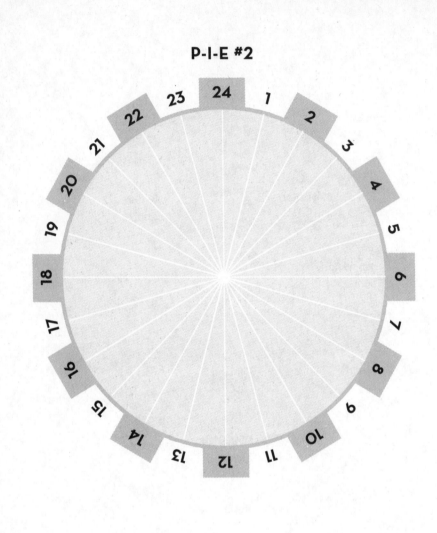

P-I-E #3

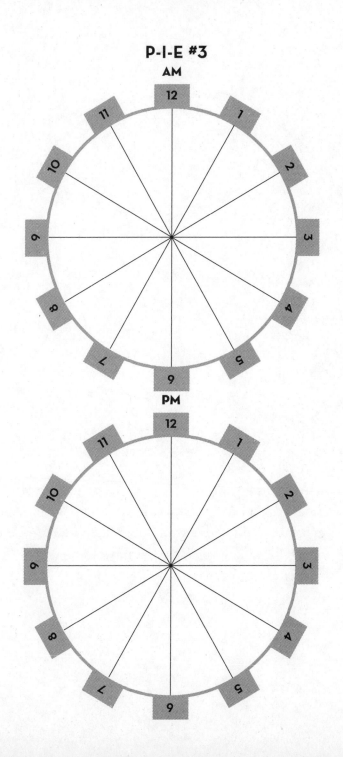

P-I-E #4

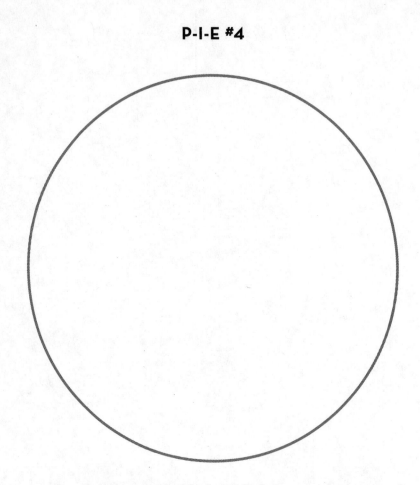

Here is a completely blank P-I-E for you to organize and fill in to help you plan—or record—your daily, weekly, or even your annual PIE (prioritize, initiate, evaluate).

About the Author

Jan Yager, Ph.D. is the author of more than 40 award-winning books translated into 34 language including 6 on time management: *Creative Time Management*; *Put More Time on Your Side*; *Work Less, Do More: The 7-Day Productivity Makeover*; *Creative Time Management for the New Millennium*; *365 Daily Affirmations for Time Management*; and *Delivering Time Management to IT Professionals: A Trainer's Manual*. Her other titles include *Friendshifts*; *When Friendship Hurts*; *365 Daily Affirmations for Happiness*; *The Fast Track Guide to Losing Weight and Keeping It Off*; *The Fast Track Guide to Speaking in Public*; *125 Ways to Meet the Love of Your Life*; and *Road Signs on Life's Journey*. A strong advocate of work-life balance, Jan has been happily married since 1984 to Fred Yager. They have two grown sons and a grandson. For more on Jan, go to: www.drjanyager.com. To book Jan for speaking engagements, contact your favorite speaker bureau or write to her at: jyager@aol.com.